T H E
Cornerstone
A N T H O L O G Y

WORKBOOK

Eden Force Eskin

GLOBE BOOK COMPANY
Englewood Cliffs, N.J.

EDEN FORCE ESKIN, co-author of *The Cornerstone Anthology* and *The Student's Anthology,* has been a managing editor of a school dictionary and has contributed articles to reference books on subjects that include vocabulary development, English usage and style, and research and reference skills. She received her B.A. in English and American Literature from Brandeis University.

Cover Design: Anne Ricigliano
Cover Photo: © Joe Viesti, Viesti Associates, Inc.

Illustrators: Bert Dodson: 4; Joseph Forte: 11; Bill Angressano: 14, 76; Virginia Arnold: 74; Ted Burwell: 18, 19, 67; Laura Lee Cundiff: 62; Erikson Studios: 6, 12, 16, 50, 54, 66, 73, 92; Julie Evans: 33; Jeff Fischer: 38; Eileen McKeating: 36; Neal McPheeters: 46, 64; Linda Miyamoto: 87, 88; Joanne Pappas: 81; Don Schlegel: 23, 31, 42, 71; Clare Sieffert: 52; Gerald Smith: 58; Cindy Spenser: 21, 44, 84; Kimanne Ulher: 16; Jean and Mou-Sien Tseng: 80.

ISBN: 0-83590-063-0

PRINTED IN THE UNITED STATES OF AMERICA
10 9 8 7

Globe Book Company
A Division of Simon & Schuster
Englewood Cliffs, New Jersey

CONTENTS

The exercises in this book accompany selections in *The Cornerstone Anthology*.

Your Reading History   1
Getting Started/Skimming the Textbook   2

UNIT 1   AMERICAN EXPERIENCE

MAMA AND PAPA/Word Mastery Exercises 3
   Understanding Character Clues   4
THE FIRST DAY/Word Mastery Exercises... 5
   Reading a Table   6
HARRIET TUBMAN, LIBERATOR/Word Mastery Exercises........................... 8
   Do You Know What Is Important in a Story?   9
   Fill in the Blanks   10
DAVY CROCKETT, FRONTIER FIGHTER/Word Mastery Exercises 11
   Reading a Map of the Alamo   12
THE PONY EXPRESS/Word Mastery Exercises 14
   Skimming to Find Information   15
SHOES FOR HECTOR/Word Mastery Exercises 16
   Multiple Meanings   17
SPLIT CHERRY TREE/Word Mastery Exercise..18
   Identifying Standard, Informal, and Slang Usages   19
   Similes and Metaphors   20

UNIT 2   SEARCHING FOR YOURSELF

THE CONFIDENCE GAME/Word Mastery Exercise 21
   Distinguishing Words That Are Often Confused   22
THICKER THAN WATER/Word Mastery Exercises 23
   Applying Information from a Chart   24
   Recognizing Kinds of Conflict   25
THE KIND OF MAN SHE COULD LOVE/Word Mastery Exercises 26
   Building Vocabulary with Prefixes   27
   Identifying Similes and Metaphors   28
THE BUTTERFLY AND THE CATERPILLAR/Rhyme Schemes....................29
   Identifying Rhythms   30
LATHER AND NOTHING ELSE/Word Mastery Exercise............................31
   Working with Suffixes   32
AQUÍ SE HABLA ESPAÑOL/Word Mastery Exercises..............................33
   Building Words with Combining Forms   34
   Elements of a Plot   35
BLIND SUNDAY/Word Mastery Exercise...36
   Homographs   37

UNIT 3   MONSTERS AND MYSTERIES

STALEY FLEMING'S HALLUCINATION/Word Mastery Exercise....................38
   Fun with Puns   39
   Using a Pronunciation Key   40
PERSEUS AND MEDUSA/Word Mastery Exercise......................................42
   Following Directions   43
THESEUS AND THE MINOTAUR/Word Mastery Exercise 44
   Personification   45

THE OPEN WINDOW/Word Mastery Exercise..46
    Compare and Contrast 47
    Summarizing 48
THE TEN-ARMED MONSTER OF NEWFOUNDLAND/Word Mastery Exercise......49
    Matching the Picture to the Description 50
PRONE/Word Mastery Exercise...52
    Determining Time Order 53
    Understanding Spatial Order 54

UNIT 4   TRYING HARDER

MY HERO/Word Mastery Exercise..56
    Making Inferences 57
OOKA AND THE STOLEN SMELL/Word Mastery Exercise......................58
    Distinguishing Sensory Images 59
    Identifying Elements of a Short Story 60
THE KICK/Word Mastery Exercise..62
    Recognizing the Author's Purpose 63
DEAR LOVEY HART, I AM DESPERATE/Word Mastery Exercise 64
    Writing a Business Letter 65
    Reading a Pie Graph 66
THE WOLF OF THUNDER MOUNTAIN/Word Mastery Exercise.................67
    Using Research Skills 68
    Recognizing Cause and Effect 70
THE FINISH OF PATSY BARNES/Word Mastery Exercise 71
    Outlining 72

UNIT 5   GREAT IDEAS

THE SUBSTANCE AND THE SHADOW/Word Mastery Exercise..................74
    Identifying Topic and Theme 75
THE MAN WHO WAS A HORSE/Word Mastery Exercise.....................76
    Distinguishing Between Fact and Opinion 77
    Designing a Cattle Brand 78
AMELIA'S BLOOMERS/Word Mastery Exercise.............................79
    Words from People's Names 80
THE PARABLE OF THE EAGLE/Word Mastery Exercise......................81
    Identifying the Moral 82
THE PATHWAY FROM SLAVERY TO FREEDOM/Word Mastery Exercise...........84
    Recognizing Settings 85
    Proofreading 86
THE BIG WAVE/Word Mastery Exercise..................................87
    Recognizing Literary Genres 88
    Paraphrasing to Change Play Forms to Narrative 90
    Reviewing Important Ideas 91
    Reviewing Literary Terms 92

Your Reading History

> In order to help you with reading this year, your teacher needs to know something about you. Complete this page as honestly and carefully as you can by filling in the lines and checking the boxes.

Name _____

Address _____

School attended last year _____ Grade _____

How much trouble do you have in each of the following areas?

	None	Little	Some	A Lot
Knowing word meanings				
Figuring out meanings of new words				
Understanding what you read				
Remembering what you read				
Reading easily and rapidly				
Keeping your mind on the job				

1. Have you had your eyes tested within the last year? _____

2. Do you wear glasses for reading? _____

3. Out of school, how much time do you spend reading on your own?

    □ A lot   □ Some   □ Little   □ Almost none

4. What kind of reading do you like best? For instance, you might answer "Car magazines, such as *Road & Track*" or "Mysteries, such as the Alfred Hitchcock collections."

   _____

5. Which *one* book or story that you read within the last year do you remember best?

   _____

   Describe it as completely as you can.

   _____

   _____

   _____

Getting Started

> There's an old saying, "You can't tell a book by its cover." This statement is certainly true. First of all, to get acquainted with *The Cornerstone Anthology*, you have to open the book and look through it by skimming. **Skimming** means glancing through or reading something quickly. Skimming the table of contents, the index, and the rest of the book will give you an idea of what's in the text.

Directions: To answer the questions below, first look at the table of contents, the index, and certain other pages in the textbook. Then fill in the blanks. Work as rapidly and accurately as you can.

1. How many units are in the book?

   _____

2. What is the title of Unit 4?

   _____

3. What story begins on page 285?

   _____

4. In addition to fiction, what other kinds of literature does the book contain? (Name at least two kinds.)

   _____

5. Find the story called "Shoes for Hector." How many pages are in the story?

   _____

6. Does the book contain any poems by Robert Frost? If so, on what page?

   _____

7. Who wrote a poem called "Who Has Seen the Wind?"?

   _____

8. Does the book contain a story called "The Open Window"? If so, on what page does it start? (Caution: Look under "O" for "Open," not under "T" for "The.")

   _____

9. Is the selection called "The Man Who Was a Horse" *fiction* or *nonfiction?*

   _____

10. What is the first line of the poem "Things"?

    _____

11. What does the Glossary of Terms on pages 394–395 contain?

    _____

12. What does a **boldfaced** page number mean in the Index of Authors and Titles on pages 399–400?

    _____

Bonus Question: In what year did Langston Hughes die?

_____

Word Mastery Exercises

A. Directions: Circle the letter of the word or phrase that best defines each of the words from "Mama and Papa" printed in *italics* below. Use the context of each word to help determine its meaning.

1. She wrote and produced *solemn* plays rather than light comedies for the theater club.

    (a) very serious   (b) very childish   (c) very funny

2. The children thought of the *boarders* as part of the family.

    (a) nearby neighbors   (b) people who own a house
    (c) people who pay to live in a house

3. After their father had been *swindled,* the ladies found that they could not afford to live as they once had.

    (a) murdered   (b) cheated   (c) sick for a long time

4. The *aviator* took people for exciting rides on weekends.

    (a) ship's captain   (b) airplane pilot
    (c) amusement park owner

5. Their voices grew *shrill* when they began to argue.

    (a) deep and angry   (b) hoarse from screaming   (c) high and sharp

Homophones are words that sound alike but have different meanings and different spellings. For example, *dear* and *deer* are homophones. Getting homophones mixed up is a common cause of spelling errors.

B. Directions: Decide which word in parentheses is the correct missing word. Then write the word in the blank.

6. The napkins had fancy _____ of lace. (borders, boarders)

7. The former policeman was a _____ in their home. (border, boarder)

8. When the women were young and lovely, they were considered to be great _____ . (bells, belles)

9. The church _____ ring out the hours and half hours. (bells, belles)

10. _____ were many people who came to the house to listen to the music. (Their, There)

Understanding Character Clues

(Keyed to "Mama and Papa" Pages 2–5)

Understanding the characters, or people, in a story is an important part of understanding the story. Most authors don't tell you everything about a character. Instead, they give you clues so that you, the reader, can figure out what the character is like.

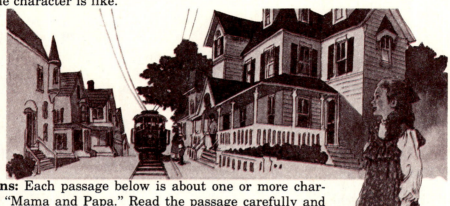

Directions: Each passage below is about one or more characters in "Mama and Papa." Read the passage carefully and use the clues to figure out something about the characters. Circle the letter of the *one* sentence after each passage that best describes the character or characters.

1. Little by little, the foreignness had disappeared from the family's life. Mama and Papa seldom spoke Norwegian anymore.

   (a) Mama and Papa studied foreign languages in school.
   (b) Mama and Papa were probably born in Norway.
   (c) Mama and Papa ran a boardinghouse for foreigners.

2. Mr. Grady often gave the Randolph sisters peppermints. They never told him that they did not like the taste of peppermint.

   (a) The Randolph sisters did not want to hurt Mr. Grady's feelings.
   (b) The Randolph sisters were too fussy.
   (c) The Randolph sisters did not like Mr. Grady.

3. Christine and Nels brought their friends to the house and considered themselves lucky that they didn't have to entertain in small apartments.

   (a) Christine and Nels were not happy with their home.
   (b) Christine and Nels lived in a small apartment.
   (c) Christine and Nels enjoyed bringing their friends home.

4. Papa sat up eagerly when Mr. Kenmore offered to take him up in an airplane.

   (a) Papa wanted to go for a ride in an airplane.
   (b) Papa thought that airplanes were too dangerous to ride in.
   (c) Papa thought that airplanes didn't work.

5. When Mama did not encourage Papa to fly, Mr. Kenmore started to say something more about flying. Then Mrs. Kenmore asked him to stop asking Papa to fly.

   (a) Mrs. Kenmore did not like Mr. Kenmore to fly.
   (b) Mrs. Kenmore did not like Mama and Papa.
   (c) Mrs. Kenmore did not want to cause trouble between Mama and Papa.

Word Mastery Exercises

A. Directions: Circle the letter of the word or phrase that best defines each of the words from "The First Day" printed in *italics* below. Use the context of each word to help determine its meaning.

1. His friends did not *begrudge* him his good luck at finding a job.
   - (a) feel angry and jealous at
   - (b) encourage to have
   - (c) understand the reason for

2. The company *guaranteed* that its hats would not wear out for a year.
   - (a) refused to say
   - (b) promised
   - (c) hoped

3. Most of the people who landed in America that day were *greenhorns*.
   - (a) new people in a country
   - (b) uneducated people
   - (c) farmers

4. He was worried about his *reputation* after people began to say mean things about him.
   - (a) health
   - (b) chance of earning money
   - (c) opinion others had of him

5. He made himself understood with *gestures* and sounds.
   - (a) hand motions
   - (b) dictionaries
   - (c) dances

> **Synonyms** are words that mean the same thing or nearly the same thing. When you replace a word with its synonym, you don't change the meaning of a sentence.

B. Directions: A **synonym** is a word that has the same or nearly the same meaning as another word. Each sentence below is followed by three words. Circle the one that is a synonym for the word in *italics*.

6. When the boat neared land, the engines *halted*.
   - (a) roared
   - (b) started
   - (c) stopped

7. He was *content* to eat his cheese and olives.
   - (a) satisfied
   - (b) unhappy
   - (c) hungry

8. He *twirled* the hat around on his finger.
   - (a) spun
   - (b) waved
   - (c) rubbed

9. The man wanted to *trade* hats with the sailor.
   - (a) sell
   - (b) exchange
   - (c) buy

10. He was very good at designing leather *ornaments*.
    - (a) patterns
    - (b) decorations
    - (c) handles

Reading a Table

(Keyed to "The First Day" Pages 8–13)

Many people who live in the United States were born in other countries. Like the hero of "The First Day," they came to find a better life. The table on this page shows the number of people who came to America from different parts of the world between 1870 and 1970. The information was put together for the 200th birthday of the United States in 1976.

To read a table, you find the places where the columns down meet the rows across. Often it is helpful to use rulers or pieces of paper to follow the columns and rows. Practice finding information on the table. Answer this question: How many people born in Asia lived in the United States in 1910? To get the answer, find the row labeled "Asia." Then find the column labeled "1910." Follow the row across and the column down until they meet. The answer is 191,484.

U.S. Foreign-Born Population, by Region of Birth, 1870-1970

	Northwestern Europe	Central and Eastern Europe	Southern Europe	Other Europe	Asia	Americas	All Other
1870	3,124,638	1,784,449	25,853	1,678	64,565	551,335	14,711
1880	3,494,484	2,187,776	58,265	3,786	107,630	807,230	20,772
1890	4,380,752	3,420,648	206,648	12,579	113,396	1,088,245	27,311
1900	4,202,683	4,136,640	530,200	2,251	120,248	1,317,380	31,868
1910	4,239,067	6,014,028	1,525,875	12,871	191,484	1,489,231	43,330
1920	3,830,94	6,134,845	1,911,213	5,901	237,950	1,727,017	73,672
1930	3,728,050	5,897,799	2,106,295	16,255	275,665	2,102,209	77,876
1950	NA	NA	NA	185,685	275,990	1,655,324	202,723
1960	1,973,025	3,717,907	1,528,473	14,320	499,312	1,860,809	144,245
1970	1,536,722	2,811,094	1,343,510	20,700	824,887	2,616,391	465,998

Notes   NA means "not available." Dates by country of birth are not available for 1940. The total number of foreign-born persons living in the United States in 1940 was 11,656,641.

Directions: Answer the questions below by using the table. (Read the notes at the bottom of the table, too.) Circle the letter of each correct answer.

1. In which of the following years did the greatest number of people from Northwestern Europe live in the United States?

    (a) 1910   (b) 1930   (c) 1970

2. From which part of Europe did the greatest number of people living in the United States in 1930 come?

    (a) Northwestern Europe   (b) Central and Eastern Europe   (c) Southern Europe

3. How many people from Asia lived in the United States in 1950?

    (a) 185,685   (b) 275,665   (c) 275,990

4. From which region did the largest number of foreign-born people living in the United States in 1970 come?

    (a) Northwestern Europe   (b) Central and Eastern Europe   (c) The Americas

5. From which region did *fewer* foreign-born people living in the United States come in 1970 than in 1870?

    (a) Northwestern Europe   (b) Asia   (c) The Americas

6. What does "NA" mean in this table?

    (a) North America   (b) new addition   (c) not available

7. Which of the following statements would be correct for the foreign-born people from the Americas?

    (a) There were more people from the Americas in 1960 than in 1930.
    (b) The number of people from the Americas in 1970 was double the number in 1960.
    (c) In 1970, there was a larger number of people from the Americas than in any other year.

8. What was the first year that the number of people from the Americas was greater than one million?

    (a) 1880   (b) 1890   (c) 1900

9. In what year did the greatest total number of foreign-born people live in the United States?

    (a) 1910   (b) 1930   (c) The table does not give this information.

10. The table shows every ten years from 1870 to 1970 except for one. Which one is missing?

    (a) 1860   (b) 1930   (c) 1940

Bonus Questions:

11. How many foreign-born people lived in the United States in 1930? _____

12. What was the total number of people from all parts of Europe living in the United States in 1960? _____

Word Mastery Exercises

A. Directions: Circle the letter of the word or phrase that best defines each of the words from "Harriet Tubman, Liberator" printed in *italics* below. Use the context of each word to help determine its meaning.

1. She *determined* that she would do everything she could to gain her freedom.

   (a) decided   (b) feared   (c) hoped

2. They *pursued* the runaway slave with dogs.

   (a) greeted   (b) helped   (c) chased

3. The brave woman helped many escape from *bondage*.

   (a) injuries   (b) sales tax   (c) slavery

4. Not everybody who read the stories had real *sentiments* against slavery.

   (a) silly ideas   (b) feelings   (c) protection

5. People gave her their *heartfelt* thanks for her help.

   (a) honest   (b) not very real   (c) written

> **Antonyms** are words that have opposite meanings. For example, *good* and *bad* are antonyms. When you replace a word with its antonym, you change the meaning to the opposite.

B. Directions: Decide which word from the word box is the *antonym* of the word in *italics* in each sentence. Write the word on the answer blank.

danger	differences	followed	freedom	succeeded

6. She wanted to escape from *slavery* to _____ .

7. Many people who left the _____ of the slave areas escaped to the *safety* of Canada.

8. She *led* those who gladly _____ her on the Underground Railroad.

9. She _____ in all her rescues and never *failed* to help the runaways escape.

10. Frederick Douglass commented on both the _____ and the *similarities* between himself and Harriet Tubman.

Do You Know What Is Important in a Story?

(Keyed to "Harriet Tubman, Liberator" Pages 24–29)

Some details make a big difference in a story. Other details are interesting, but changing them would not change the story. When you read a story, it is important to see which details are necessary to make the story work. For example, an important detail in "Harriet Tubman, Liberator" is the fact that she was a slave. If she were not a slave, the story would not have happened the way it did. The author also tells us that she was homely. That does not make a big difference in the story.

Directions: Decide which of the following sentences tells us something that is important to the story "Harriet Tubman, Liberator." Write *I* on the line next to an important detail. If the detail is not important to the story, write *N* on the line.

Then pick one of the sentences you marked *I* and explain why it is important to the story.

_____ 1. Harriet Tubman was married.

_____ 2. When she escaped, she followed the North Star to find her way.

_____ 3. Sometimes she used songs as messages.

_____ 4. The first river she reached was called the Choptank River.

_____ 5. She did not know how to read a map.

_____ 6. Harriet Tubman wanted to free her family and friends.

_____ 7. Nobody that Harriet Tubman helped was ever captured.

_____ 8. The name of one slave she helped was Charles Nalle.

_____ 9. She helped more than 300 slaves escape to freedom.

_____ 10. She died in Auburn, New York.

Sentence number _____ is important to the story because _____

_____

_____

_____

_____

Fill in the Blanks

(Keyed to "Harriet Tubman, Liberator" Pages 24–29)

Directions: Here is a description of a group of slaves escaping by the Underground Railroad. Ten words are missing. Your job is to decide which of the four words at the right belongs in each blank. First, read the whole selection to get an idea of the story. Then go back and write the correct words on the answer blanks. After you are finished, read the story once more to see if it makes sense with the words you wrote.

They could hear someone _____ (1) the song "Follow the Drinking Gourd." They knew that it was a _____ (2) message telling them to follow the Big Dipper and the North Star. The small group of _____ (3) stole away from the plantation. They kept themselves in the _____ (4) because they did not want to be seen in the moonlight. The "conductor" met them as they _____ (5) the woods. He led them to a river where they _____ (6) for many miles in the water. When they reached an old barn, they went _____ (7) and stayed there for the night.

They traveled for many more nights. One day the conductor told them to look for a _____ (8) of a slave on the lawn. If there was a flag in its _____ (9), it was safe to go into the house. If there wasn't, they must keep going. There was a flag, and they found a _____ (10) place to stay in the house. The next day, they crossed over into a free state.

1. walking, singing, knowing, believing

2. written, false, big, secret

3. slaves, owners, watchmen, artists

4. sun, shadows, light, truck

5. chopped, smelled, reached, heard

6. walked, sang, screamed, sat

7. outside, inside, away, across

8. movie, shoe, smile, statue

9. hand, camera, book, message

10. dangerous, safe, green, scratchy

Word Mastery Exercises

(Keyed to "Davy Crockett, Frontier Fighter" Pages 34–40)

A. Directions: Circle the letter of the word or phrase that best defines each of the words from "Davy Crockett, Frontier Fighter" printed in *italics* below. Use the context of each word to help determine its meaning.

1. Davy Crockett's many amazing deeds showed that he had a lot of *gumption*.

    (a) weakness   (b) money
    (c) courage

2. People thought so much of his political sense that they elected him to the state *legislature*.

    (a) lawmaking group   (b) university   (c) hunters' group

3. He *shinnied* up a tree to see the land around it.

    (a) chopped   (b) jumped   (c) climbed

4. They *ambled* through the field of wheat.

    (a) ran   (b) walked slowly   (c) crawled

5. He could hear the *whir* of birds' wings.

    (a) humming sound   (b) slapping   (c) feathers

B. Directions: Below are some more homophones. (If you don't remember what homophones are, look back at page 3.) Each sentence has *two* homophones. Decide which word belongs in each blank, and write the correct word in the blank.

6. _____ are some good songs for you to _____ .

    (hear, here)

7. He caught a _____ with his _____ hands.

    (bare, bear)

8. He _____ go into the forest and chop _____ .

    (wood, would)

9. It was only the _____ of a tree, _____ a raccoon.

    (knot, not)

10. The _____ in the tree was large enough for a _____

    family of squirrels.   (hole, whole)

Reading a Map of the Alamo

(Keyed to "Davy Crockett, Frontier Fighter" Pages 34–40)

Davy Crockett died after fighting the battle of the Alamo on March 6, 1836. He was one of many famous people who fought that day against a Mexican army led by Mexico's president, General Santa Anna. Two other famous men who died there were William Barret Travis and James Bowie.

Although the small Texan group of 188 men were no match for the 1,500 Mexican soldiers, they fought bravely. All those who defended the Alamo died. After the Mexicans won the battle, "Remember the Alamo!" became a cry that brought Texans and Americans together to defeat Santa Anna and the Mexican troops 46 days later. Texas became an independent country. In 1845 Texas joined the United States.

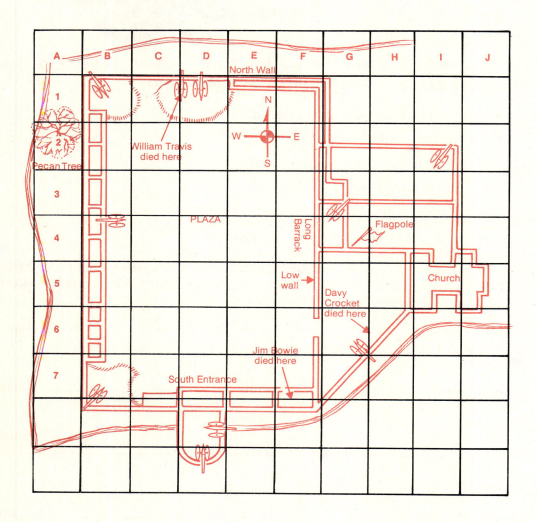

The map on page 12 shows the Alamo, the fort where Davy Crockett died fighting against a Mexican army in 1836. Like many maps, it is divided into columns going down and rows going across. Using the columns and rows helps you find places on the map. Letters and numbers are given to help you locate the place you want. Use them the same way you used letters and numbers to read a table. Find the letter of the column down and follow it. Then find the number of the row across. The place where the column and row meet is the place you are looking for.

A. Directions: Use the map on page 12 to answer the questions below. Find the place on the map by using the letter and number. Tell what is shown at each of these places.

1. A 2 _____

2. I 5 _____

3. G 6 _____

4. F 4 _____

5. C 1 _____

B. Directions: Give the letter and number for each place named below.

6. South Entrance _____ _____

7. Place where Jim Bowie died _____ _____

8. Low wall _____ _____

9. North wall (give just the number) _____

10. Long Barracks (give just the letter) _____

Word Mastery Exercises

(Keyed to "The Pony Express" Pages 52–54)

A. Directions: Circle the letter of the word or phrase that best defines each of the words from "The Pony Express" printed in *italics* below. Use the context of each word to help determine its meaning.

1. The small ponies were chosen for speed and *endurance*.

   (a) high spirits   (b) ability to last   (c) hard hooves

2. Pony riders had to dress with the *utmost* care to keep their clothing from slowing them down.

   (a) greatest   (b) least   (c) professional tailor's

3. Everybody stood around admiring the spirited *steed*.

   (a) cowboy   (b) team   (c) horse

4. We *strained* our necks to watch the rider whiz by.

   (a) stretched   (b) wrapped   (c) injured

5. She picked up some *fragments* of a jar that she found on the ground.

   (a) small pieces   (b) colored labels   (c) wrapped candy

B. Directions: In the letter below, five words are spelled wrong. Each wrong spelling gives the homophone instead of the correct word. Find them and cross them out. Write the correct spelling above the word you have crossed out.

```
       Deer Marty,

          Did you get the letter I cent you last

       weak? Please right to me and tell me how you

       are. All your friends hear are fine.

                              Your friend,

                              Sam
```

Skimming to Find Information

(Keyed to "The Pony Express" Pages 52–54)

When you read stories, you usually read slowly and carefully to understand what the story is about. There are times, however, when you just need to skim. When you **skim,** you look for information, such as a name or date. For example, you might need to know the date of some important event. To do this you skim until you find the information you need.

Directions: Read the questions. Then skim the encyclopedia article to find the answers. Write your answers on the blanks.

PONY EXPRESS   The pony express was a United States mail service that began on April 3, 1860. It was set up to carry mail between St. Joseph, Missouri, and Sacramento, California, a distance of nearly 2,000 miles. Mail was carried on horseback by a series of riders. Each rode about 75 miles and then handed the mail to the next rider. The riders changed horses every 10–15 miles. It usually took about eight days for the mail to make the trip from St. Joseph to Sacramento. When the service began, the mail was carried once a week. Later it was carried twice a week. The mail was lost only once in the 16 months that the system lasted.

The pony express replaced the slower systems of carrying mail by stagecoach, wagons, and ships. The invention of the telegraph ended the need for the pony express. Pony express service ended gradually after October 24, 1861, when telegraph lines reached California. Even though it lasted a short time, the pony express lived on in stories and legends.

1. When did pony express service start?

_____

2. When did it end?

_____

3. What invention made the pony express unnecessary?

_____

4. How many months did the pony express last?

_____

5. Between what two cities did pony express mail travel?

_____

6. What was the total distance covered by the pony express service?

_____

7. About how often did a rider change horses?

_____

8. How long did it take the mail to make the trip by pony express?

_____

Word Mastery Exercises

(Keyed to "Shoes for Hector" Pages 59–63)

A. Directions: Circle the letter of the word or phrase that best defines each of the words from "Shoes for Hector" printed in *italics* below. Use the context of each word to help determine its meaning.

1. His uncle *gestured* to him to look at something.
   (a) shouted   (b) asked   (c) motioned

2. His father was *laid off* because business was slow.
   (a) punished   (b) put out of work for a while   (c) fired

3. The angry child sat in her room and *sulked*.
   (a) acted moodily   (b) shouted loudly   (c) cried hard

4. The *inscription* on the watch showed his name and the date.
   (a) face   (b) hands   (c) writing or engraving

5. The room was decorated with *multicolored* balloons.
   (a) many-colored   (b) very brightly colored   (c) red and yellow

> A **rebus** is a riddle or puzzle in which pictures replace some of the words. The pictures may be of the words, or they may be homophones for the words. For example, instead of the word *be* there may be a picture of a bee or the letter *B*.

B. Directions: Figure out what the rebus puzzle below says and write it on the blanks.

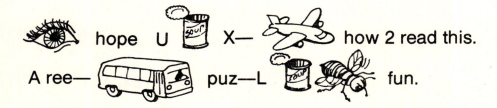

_____

_____

_____

Multiple Meanings

(Keyed to "Shoes for Hector" Pages 59–63)

When you look up a word in a dictionary, you may find that different meanings are given. Many words have more than one meaning. After you find the word, you must decide which definition is the one you need. One way to decide is to study the **context,** the words around the word you are looking up. Then see which meaning fits best.

Directions: Decide which numbered definition from the dictionary entry is the best one for the sentence. Write the number of the definition on the answer blank.

ex·er·cise (ek′s r-sīz′) *noun* **1.** an act of using: *the exercise of a president's power.* **2.** an activity done to improve strength, muscles, staying power, or flexibility: *Swimming is good exercise.* **3.** a lesson or problem that is supposed to build skill: *The teacher gave us vocabulary exercises for homework.* **4. exercises** special ceremony: *graduation exercises.* —*verb* **ex er cised, ex er cis ing 5.** to put into use: *to exercise one's power as ruler.* **6.** to do physical exercises: *She exercises to music every morning.* **7.** to give physical exercise to: *He exercises his dog in the schoolyard.*

pain (pān) *noun* **1.** a suffering or hurt in the body that comes from injury or disease: *a sharp pain in the side.* **2.** a suffering in mind or feelings; great distress: *the pain of losing a pet.* **3. pains** extra effort, care, or trouble: *She takes pains to do the job well.* —*verb* **4.** to cause a physical feeling of hurt: *The old injury pains him in cold weather.* **5.** to cause to suffer: *It pains me to see you suffer.*

_____ **1.** At what time will the *exercises* take place for the award winners?

_____ **2.** Do you like to *exercise?*

_____ **3.** Bicycling is my favorite *exercise.*

_____ **4.** People who do not *exercise* their rights may lose them.

_____ **5.** The first sign of the illness was a *pain* in her back.

_____ **6.** He took great *pains* to make his watch work again.

_____ **7.** It *pains* me to tell you the bad news.

_____ **8.** He cannot stand the *pain* of another failure.

Word Mastery Exercise

(Keyed to "Split Cherry Tree" Pages 66–78)

Directions: Circle the letter of the word or phrase that best defines each of the words from "Split Cherry Tree" printed in *italics* below. Use the context of each word to help determine its meaning.

1. The farmer kept *fodder* in a storage barn.

    (a) saddles for riding   (b) farm tools   (c) food for cattle

2. His school subjects included social studies, *biology,* and math.

    (a) study of books   (b) study of living things   (c) study of machines

3. The audience *plagued* the speaker with silly questions.

    (a) bothered   (b) helped   (c) wrote letters to

4. He *ransacked* his room to find his wallet.

    (a) cleaned up   (b) searched through   (c) went into

5. The pirates *pillaged* all the towns on the coast.

    (a) robbed and destroyed   (b) visited for fun   (c) built seaports in

6. The price of the camera was very *steep*.

    (a) fair   (b) cheap   (c) expensive

7. The students *dissected* frogs in science class.

    (a) cut up   (b) watched   (c) drew pictures of

8. The old tree was *gnarled* and rough.

    (a) strong   (b) full of holes   (c) twisted

Bonus Activity: Choose two of the words above. Write a sentence for each of them.

9. _____

10. _____

18 / THE CORNERSTONE ANTHOLOGY

Identifying Standard, Informal, and Slang Usages

(Keyed to "Split Cherry Tree" Pages 66–78)

Some ways of speaking and writing fit any situation. It doesn't matter if you are talking or writing to a friend, a teacher, or the president of the country. Words and sentences that fit almost any use are part of **standard** language.

Other words are used only in more casual situations. Words and sentences of this kind are part of **informal** language.

Still another kind of language is slang. A **slang** expression may not be understood by people who have never heard it. Slang words are not "bad English," but they do not fit all situations. They are used mostly with good friends. Many slang terms do not last long. If they do, they often become part of informal language.

"Let's leave" is an example of standard English. An informal way of saying the same thing might be, "Let's get going." In slang it might be, "Let's split."

Directions: Decide which sentence is standard English, which is informal, and which is slang. Write *standard, informal,* or *slang* on the blank.

1. How's your boy? _____

2. How is your son? _____

3. How's your kid? _____

4. This is boring. _____

5. This is dullsville. _____

6. This puts me to sleep. _____

7. It was a blast. _____

8. A good time was had by all. _____

9. Everyone had a good time. _____

Similes and Metaphors

(Keyed to "Split Cherry Tree" Pages 66–78)

> Writers often use images to help us get an idea of something. Two kinds of images are used to compare one thing to another. A **simile** compares two things by using the words *as* or *like*. For example, you might say, "The basketball player is *as tall as* a pine tree" or, "The lake was *like* glass."
>
> A **metaphor** compares two things but does not use the words *as* or *like*. It says or suggests that one thing is another. For example, "His fist was a hammer."
>
> Some similes and metaphors are used so often that they are no longer interesting. "It is as white as snow" and "Her teeth are pearls" are used so commonly that we don't pay attention to them.

Directions: Finish each sentence below by writing an interesting simile or metaphor *that you have not heard often.*

1. The girl was as thin as _____ .

2. The tangled thread was a _____ .

3. The ice was like _____ .

4. Her angry words cut like _____ .

5. The starlit sky was a _____ .

6. I am as happy as _____ .

7. The moon is a _____ .

8. His hands were as rough as _____ .

9. Her eyes sparkled like _____ .

10. He is as strong as _____ .

Bonus Activity: Look over the sentences and decide which are similes and which are metaphors. Write *S* for simile or *M* for metaphor next to each sentence.

Word Mastery Exercise

(Keyed to "The Confidence Game" Pages 88–93)

Directions: Circle the letter of the word or phrase that best defines each of the words from "The Confidence Game" printed in *italics* below. Use the context of each word to help determine its meaning.

1. Having someone to race against often *motivates* a racer to try harder.

   (a) makes someone want to   (b) discourages someone from doing
   (c) teaches someone to

2. "Noses are red," she *quipped* as she looked at the room full of people with colds.

   (a) screamed   (b) stopped talking   (c) made a funny remark

3. It should be *obvious* that athletes who don't get enough sleep cannot do their best.

   (a) difficult to understand   (b) unpleasant   (c) very clear

4. His *negative* opinion of himself caused him to do badly.

   (a) looking at the worst side; not helpful
   (b) looking at the best side; very helpful
   (c) looking at a way to cheat; dishonest

5. Just before you enter a contest, think *positive* thoughts about winning.

   (a) looking at the worst side; not helpful
   (b) looking at the best side; very helpful
   (c) looking at a way to cheat; dishonest

6. The coach works out the *strategy* for the game, and the players try to follow it.

   (a) time and place   (b) careful plans for winning   (c) rules for playing

7. A *conflict* in the schedule makes it impossible for the team to play both games.

   (a) mistake   (b) disagreement   (c) trick

8. Everybody was *ecstatic* when both girls won medals.

   (a) very joyful   (b) confused   (c) surprised

Bonus Activity: Write two sentences, each of which contains a simile or a metaphor.

9. _____

10. _____

Distinguishing Words That Are Often Confused

(Keyed to "The Confidence Game" Pages 88–93)

> Some words are not true homophones, but they sound enough alike so that many people get them mixed up. Two such pairs of words are *accept/except* and *affect/effect*. The most usual meanings for these words are shown below.
>
> **accept** (ak sept′) *verb* to take or receive; to agree to; to consider to be true.
> **except** (ik sept′) *preposition* including everything but; not including.
> **affect** (ə fekt′) *verb* to act upon; to bring about a change or to influence; to pretend to be.
> **effect** (i fekt′) *noun* thing that is a result of something else; power to cause results; something done to create an impression.
>
> Notice that in the meanings given, *accept* and *affect* are verbs, or **action** words. They both begin with an *a*. The word *except* is a preposition, and *effect* is a noun.

Directions: Choose the correct word from each pair of words and write it in the answer blank.

1. It was hard for her to _____ another good swimmer on the team.   (accept, except)

2. Everyone _____ Tobi thought that the new girl would win.   (accept, except)

3. Both girls were delighted to _____ the medals for winning.   (accept, except)

4. Angela had all the racing skills _____ the ability to think positively.   (accept, except)

5. Positive thinking can _____ your chances of winning.   (affect, effect)

6. The new girl's appearance on the team had the _____ of making Tobi angry.   (affect, effect)

7. Tobi tried to create the _____ that she didn't care about having Angela on the team.   (affect, effect)

8. The only way to _____ a change in her performance was to learn positive thinking.   (affect, effect)

Word Mastery Exercises

A. Directions: Circle the letter of the word or phrase that best defines each of the words from "Thicker Than Water" printed in *italics* below. Use the context of each word to help determine its meaning.

1. A *ruptured* eardrum had kept the army from accepting Joey.

   (a) swollen   (b) broken   (c) sore

2. A boxer could have a *disability* that would keep him from fighting in a war, but it might not be serious enough to keep him from boxing.

   (a) handicap   (b) wound   (c) family problem

3. Fear of being hurt often seemed to *paralyze* Joey.

   (a) make powerless   (b) make angry   (c) make stronger

4. The boxer *feinted* with his right and punched with his left.

   (a) hit first   (b) became unconscious   (c) pretended to move

5. He *wheezed* and gasped after he was hit.

   (a) cried out   (b) breathed hard   (c) whistled

B. Directions: Decide which word in parentheses is the correct missing word. Write the word in the blank.

6. People who come into a country to live are called _____ .

   (emigrants, immigrants)

7. The manager gave him a _____ to tell him to start punching.

   (signal, single)

8. Sometimes he refused to listen to the _____ his manager gave him.   (advice, advise)

9. He began to realize that his manager was his best _____ .   (fiend, friend)

10. Some people _____ when they see blood.   (faint, feint)

Bonus Activity: Choose one of the words in parentheses above and write your own sentence using that word.

Applying Information from a Chart

(Keyed to "Thicker Than Water" Pages 96–103)

Professional boxers are divided into classes according to weight. A boxer may not weigh more than the top weight in his class. The chart below gives the names of the classes of boxers and the most any boxer in that class is allowed to weigh.

Name of Class	Top Weight for Class (in pounds)
Flyweight	112
Bantamweight	118
Featherweight	126
Lightweight	135
Welterweight	147
Middleweight	160
Light Heavyweight	175
Heavyweight	more than 175 pounds

A. Directions: Below is a list of men who want to be boxers. Next to each name is the man's weight. Decide which class each belongs in and write the name of the class on the blank.

1. Joe Sanchez (134) _____

2. Henry Jones (158) _____

3. Mike Lyons (112) _____

4. Bill Murphy (168) _____

5. Rafael Ramos (181) _____

B. Directions: The boxers listed below won titles in different boxing classes. Use the name of the class to figure out the most each boxer could have weighed at his winning bout. Write the top weight on the blank.

6. Eddie Mustava Muhammad, Light Heavyweight _____

7. Angel Espada, Welterweight _____

8. Willy Pep, Featherweight _____

9. Bud Smith, Lightweight _____

10. Hugo Corro, Middleweight _____

Bonus Activity: Write a sentence telling why you think fighters must fight others of about the same weight.

Recognizing Kinds of Conflict

(Keyed to "Thicker Than Water" Pages 96–103)

As you know, there are three basic kinds of conflict in a story. These are (a) conflicts between people or groups of people, (b) conflicts between people and things (natural forces, objects, sickness, etc.), and (c) conflicts within a person.

Directions: Read each sentence below and decide which kind of conflict it shows. Then write the letter *a*, *b*, or *c* in the blank to tell which kind of conflict it is.

_____ 1. Joey has to decide whether he will fight or run away.

_____ 2. When the other boxer starts fighting harder, Joey tries to beat him.

_____ 3. Mary is lost in a boat at sea and must battle heavy waves and cold weather before she reaches shore.

_____ 4. Jeff must find a way to get out of the locked room before the poisonous gas kills him.

_____ 5. The witch has imprisoned the boy, and he must escape before she turns him into a toad.

_____ 6. The Star Raiders have to fight the Evil Ones to save the universe.

_____ 7. The space travelers must find a way to keep the black hole from swallowing them and destroying them.

_____ 8. Iflim must decide whether he is brave enough to join the crew of the spaceship or remain where he is.

_____ 9. Betty Sue knows who has stolen the money, but she is not sure whether she should tell the sheriff.

_____ 10. Can the small group of campers find a way to survive the hurricane?

_____ 11. The robbers threaten Mrs. MacGrath, but she beats them with her cane.

_____ 12. Marcia must decide whether to run for Congress or to help the candidate her party has chosen.

Word Mastery Exercises

(Keyed to "The Kind of Man She Could Love" Pages 106–111)

A. Directions: Circle the letter of the word or phrase that best defines each of the words from "The Kind of Man She Could Love" printed in *italics* below. Use the context of each word to help determine its meaning.

1. The young man kept a *genteel* appearance even though he did not have much money.

    (a) tame   (b) expensive   (c) well-mannered

2. The young actress loved being in the *limelight* and enjoyed the audience's applause.

    (a) center of attention   (b) neon lighting   (c) traffic lights

3. The *razzle-dazzle* of the heart of the city at night attracted the young couple.

    (a) glamour   (b) confusion   (c) noise

4. She thanked him *heartily* for helping her when she was unable to walk.

    (a) with great pain   (b) with sadness   (c) with enthusiasm

5. He took his new friend to a restaurant that had the *distinction* of serving fine food as musicians played.

    (a) expensive menu   (b) special quality   (c) newspaper ads

B. Directions: Choose the word from the word box that best fits each blank below. Some words in the box will not be used.

affect	genteel	hardly	quiet
effect	gentle	heartily	quite

6. His boasting had the _____ of making her decide he was not a very interesting person.

7. The kitten was _____ , but the mother cat was fierce.

8. The tiny woman was _____ taller than his little sister.

9. She told him she was _____ grateful for his help.

10. She knew that it was considered not _____ nice to talk to a stranger.

Building Vocabulary with Prefixes

(Keyed to "The Kind of Man She Could Love" Pages 106–111)

> A **prefix** is a word part that may be attached to the beginning of a word. Adding the prefix changes the meaning of the word. For example, the prefix *re-*, meaning "again," can be attached to the word *fill*. *Refill* means "fill again." The word to which a prefix is attached is called a *base word*.
>
> When you know the meanings of prefixes and the meanings of the base words, you can figure out the meanings of the words made by combining them.

Directions: Use the meanings given below for each prefix to help you figure out the meaning of the word in *italics* in each sentence below. Write a definition of that word on the blank. The first one has been done for you.

mis-	wrong or wrongly	*re-*	again
pre-	before	*sub-*	under, lower, lower part, or smaller part of

1. Her pen leaked and she had to *readdress* the envelope.

   To readdress means to address again.

2. They agreed not to *prejudge* the new worker.

   _____

3. The gardener had to dig down into the *subsoil* to find the problem.

   _____

4. The owner fired the coach for *mishandling* the star player.

   _____

5. The committee set up a *subcommittee* to look into the problem.

   _____

6. If you *precook* the food early in the day, it will take only a few minutes to heat it later.

   _____

7. She *reheated* the food and served it.

   _____

8. We all apologized for *misjudging* her character.

   _____

Identifying Similes and Metaphors

(Keyed to "The Kind of Man She Could Love" Pages 106–111)

Directions: Read each sentence below and circle the part that is a simile or a metaphor. (If you need to review these terms, look back at page 20.) Then tell what things are being compared in each sentence. The first one is done for you.

1. Wildflowers covered the ground like (a multicolored carpet.)

   Wildflowers are being compared to a multicolored carpet.

2. His nasty words were a swarm of bees stinging my feelings.

   _____

3. The child's kiss was a butterfly's wings on his cheek.

   _____

4. The cry echoed like a drumroll across the land.

   _____

5. The old book's pages were as crumbly as dry leaves after a drought.

   _____

6. The house smelled as stale as an uncleaned school gym.

   _____

7. The lawn mower was an angry monster roaring over the land.

   _____

8. She was as out of place as a dinosaur in a space capsule.

   _____

9. His anger was a storm threatening to destroy everything around him.

   _____

10. Her kindness soothed us like cool water on a hot day.

    _____

Rhyme Schemes

(Keyed to "The Butterfly and the Caterpillar" Pages 114–115)

Words **rhyme** when they have the same sounds at the end. They do not have to end in the same spelling, just the same sound. So *ate, wait,* and *gate* rhyme. Some words that end in the same spellings do not rhyme. For example, *rough* and *bough* do not rhyme.

Many poems rhyme, and there is a pattern to their rhyme. Most rhymes are at the ends of lines. To describe the pattern, or **rhyme scheme,** we give a different letter to each group of rhyming words. In a poem, some lines may rhyme with others, and some may not.

Directions: Use letters to show which lines rhyme. Then write the rhyme scheme on the blank next to the number. The first one is done for you.

1. _____ *a b c b* _____

The bird flew high   *a*

On a sunny day   *b*

And it sang a song   *c*

Of the glories of May.   *b*

2. _____

On a bough

He showed how

One must sing

In the spring.

3. _____

Roses are red

Violets are blue

Someone once said

That is not always true.

4. _____

They picked flowers

For many hours

But quickly sped

To a nearby shed

To escape spring showers.

5. _____

In an old wooden box

They found a red fox

Who had found a new home

Among piles of socks.

6. _____

On days that are sunny

The bees make some honey

That we'll sell for money.

7. _____

Rain, rain

On the windowpane,

Please go away

Till another day.

8. _____

Soon the green

Turns to gold—

From ages old

An autumn scene.

Bonus Question: Two of the poems on this page have the same rhyme scheme. Which two are they?

_____ and _____

Identifying Rhythms

Most poetry, like music, is based on **rhythms.** The rhythms usually have one strong beat to a **measure,** or section. Each measure usually has two or three syllables. Often you can tap or clap out a rhythm; soft clap for the weak syllables and harder clap for the stronger syllables. When rhythms are written, a dash may be used for the weak syllable and a slash for a strong one, like the following:

— / — / — / — /
I like to see it lap the miles

Sometimes lines are drawn between the measures, like this:

— / / — / / — / / — / /
I like / to see / it lap / the miles /

But many people can feel the rhythm and don't have to write it out.

Directions: Match the rhythms of each line below to the numbered line that has the same rhythm. Write the letter of the matched rhythm on the blank.

_____ 1. I like to see it lap the miles

_____ 2. I heard the skylark sing

_____ 3. His song of love

_____ 4. And find

_____ 5. Yet I creep

_____ 6. I have left you behind

_____ 7. A sense of pleasant ease on such a day

_____ 8. While I nodded, nearly napping, suddenly there came a tapping

(a) She made a sudden bound.

(b) Your comfort long, and lose your love thereby

(c) His tender notes

(d) Nowhere

(e) In the path of the past

(f) Eagerly I wished the morrow; vainly I had sought to borrow

(g) And stop to feed itself at tanks

(h) Brought thee low

Bonus Activity: Choose one of these rhythms and write a poem of two or more lines using that rhythm. Use a separate sheet of paper for poems longer than two lines.

_____

_____

Word Mastery Exercise

(Keyed to "Lather and Nothing Else" Pages 129–134)

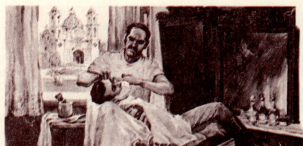

Directions: Circle the letter of the word or phrase that best defines each of the words from "Lather and Nothing Else" printed in *italics* below. Use the context of each word to help determine its meaning.

1. The barber's towel was *suspended* from a hook.

   (a) falling off   (b) hanging down   (c) taken away

2. He was too *timid* to ask any questions.

   (a) shy   (b) ignorant   (c) proud

3. At last he *ventured* some remarks about the weather and crops.

   (a) cautiously said   (b) whispered slowly   (c) announced loudly

4. The fighting had left *scanty* crops for the people to live on for the year.

   (a) a large amount of   (b) not enough of   (c) wildly growing

5. The captain's *reputation* made the barber afraid of him.

   (a) boasting and bragging   (b) guns and swords   (c) what people said about him

6. The barber often reported the soldiers' *activities* to the people in the village.

   (a) games and sports   (b) movements and actions   (c) wild behavior

7. The barber's *modesty* kept him from saying too much about himself.

   (a) lack of conceit   (b) feeling of not being good   (c) difficulty in talking

8. The captain wanted to hunt the *rebels* hiding out in the hills.

   (a) soldiers who ran from fighting   (b) robbers and murderers
   (c) people who fought his authority

9. The barber considered himself to be a *revolutionary*.

   (a) good citizen   (b) person fighting to change the government
   (c) person fighting for a democracy

10. The captain's people often *mutilated* the bodies of their prisoners.

    (a) refused to bury   (b) left out in the open   (c) cut up in a cruel way

Bonus Activity: Choose two of the words in *italics* and write one sentence using both of them.

_____

_____

Working with Suffixes

(Keyed to "Lather and Nothing Else" Pages 129–134)

A **suffix** is a word part that may be attached to the end of a word. Adding the suffix usually changes the word to a different part of speech. For example, adding the suffix *-ance* changes the verb *appear* to the noun *appearance*. Sometimes adding a suffix does not change the part of speech, but it does change the meaning. For example, adding the suffix *-er* to the noun execution changes it to the noun *executioner*, meaning "one who performs an execution." Sometimes letters are dropped or changed when adding a suffix.

When you know the meanings of the base words and the meanings of the suffixes, you can figure out the meanings of the words made by combining them.

Directions: Study the meanings for the suffixes below. Then decide which word from the word box is correct in each sentence.

-able or *-ible*   forms adjectives meaning "able to, capable of, tending to, worthy of"
-ance or *-ence*   forms nouns from verbs, meaning "condition of being"
-ment   forms nouns, meaning "action or process, condition, result of an action"
-tion   forms nouns, meaning "act of, state of being, or thing that is"

avoidable	excitable	punishable	recognizable
avoidance	excitement	punishment	recognition

1. The word that means "worthy of being punished" is _____.

2. The word that means "action of punishing" is _____.

3. The word that means "the act of recognizing" is _____.

4. The word that means "capable of being recognized" is _____.

5. The word that means "capable of being avoided" is _____.

6. The word that means "condition of being avoided" is _____.

7. The word that means "condition of being excited" is _____.

8. The word that means "tending to be excited" is _____.

Bonus Activity: Use a dictionary to find two other words with any of these suffixes. List the words and tell what they mean.

_____

_____

Word Mastery Exercises

A. Directions: Circle the letter of the word or phrase that best defines each of the words from "Aquí Se Habla Español" printed in *italics* below. Use the context of each word to help determine its meaning.

1. The picture of the Statue of Liberty *symbolized* their hopes for the future.

   (a) made unreal   (b) spoke loudly of   (c) was a sign of

2. Her *accusations* against the children were not based on any real errors.

   (a) charges of doing wrong   (b) freeing from punishment   (c) harsh punishments

3. Andrew was *bewildered* by the rapid conversation in Spanish.

   (a) confused   (b) insulted   (c) embarrassed

4. Maria's brother smiled and *ushered* the guest into the living room.

   (a) pushed   (b) led   (c) called

5. Maria did not seem to be embarrassed about her mother's *unkempt* hair.

   (a) very fancy   (b) unevenly gray   (c) not neat

B. Directions: Figure out what the common idea is in each pair of cognates and finish the sentences below. Use a dictionary if you need to.

6. The Spanish word *comprende* means "understand." The English word *comprehend* is a

   cognate. Comprehend means _____ .

7. The Spanish word *amor* means "love." The English word *amorous* means "having to do with

   _____ ."

8. The French word *amour* and the Italian word *amore* are cognates of the Spanish word

   amor. They all mean _____ .

9. The Spanish word *amigo* and the French word *ami* both mean "friend." The English

   adjective *amiable* is a cognate. Amiable means _____ .

10. The Spanish word *comenzar* means "to begin." Its English cognate *commence* means

    _____ .

Building Words with Combining Forms

(Keyed to "Aquí Se Habla Español" Pages 138–143)

> A **combining form** is a word part that can help make up other words. A combining form may go at the beginning, middle, or end of a word. Most combining forms in English come from Latin and Greek words. When you know the meanings of some of the combining forms, you can often figure out the meanings of the words they form.

Directions: Study the combining forms below. Then choose the word from the word box that best completes each sentence and write it on the answer blank.

graph, graphy writing		*phot, photo* light	
logy study of		*port* carry	
meter, metry measure, measuring		*tele* distance	
phon, phono sound		*trans* across	

graphology	phonograph	photograph	portable	telegraph
telemetry	telephone	telephoto	teleport	transport

1. The word _____ comes from combining forms meaning "carry across."

2. The word _____ comes from combining forms meaning "carry over a distance."

3. The word _____ comes from combining forms meaning "light writing."

4. The word _____ comes from combining forms meaning "writing over a distance."

5. The word _____ comes from combining forms meaning "writing sound."

6. The word _____ comes from combining forms meaning "capable of being carried."

7. The word _____ comes from combining forms meaning "sound over a distance."

8. The word _____ comes from combining forms meaning "measure over a distance."

9. The word _____ comes from combining forms meaning "light over a distance."

10. The word _____ comes from combining forms meaning "study of writing."

Bonus Activity: Find one more word with any of the combining forms on this page. On a separate sheet of paper, tell the meaning of the word and the meanings of the combining forms.

Elements of the Plot

(Keyed to "Aquí Se Habla Español" Pages 138–143)

> Many plots can be described in terms of four important ideas. They are conflict, rising action, climax (turning point), and conclusion. If you need to, review each of these terms in the Glossary of Terms, pages 394–395.

Directions: Decide which sentence fits each part of the plot for each of the stories below. Write the letter of the sentence next to the plot idea it describes.

A. The Confidence Game (pages 88–93)

(a) At the swim meet, Tobi decides to help Angela.

(b) Tobi must deal with her own jealousy.

(c) Both Tobi and Angela win the right to compete.

(d) Tobi's performance suffers and tension builds between Tobi and Angela.

_____ 1. conflict

_____ 2. rising action

_____ 3. turning point

_____ 4. conclusion

B. Thicker Than Water (pages 96–103)

(a) Joey is fighting well in a match he must win, when his opponent lands a good punch.

(b) The coach tells Joey he has his brother's blood.

(c) Joey fights back and wins the match.

(d) Joey has to overcome his desire to stop fighting when he is hit.

_____ 5. conflict

_____ 6. rising action

_____ 7. turning point

_____ 8. conclusion

C. The Kind of Man She Could Love (pages 106–111)

(a) The reader learns that Marian might have loved a man who worked hard.

(b) When Marian tells Chandler his life is useless, he does not tell her the truth.

(c) Chandler wants to impress Miss Marian.

(d) Chandler begins telling lies to make himself sound rich and important.

_____ 9. conflict

_____ 10. rising action

_____ 11. turning point

_____ 12. conclusion

Word Mastery Exercise

(Keyed to "Blind Sunday" Pages 148–172)

Directions: Circle the letter of the word or phrase that best defines each of the words from "Blind Sunday" printed in *italics* below. Use the context of each word to help determine its meaning.

1. Eileen *executed* a beautiful dive into the pool.

   (a) spoiled   (b) did   (c) stopped

2. Jeff's *encounter* with Eileen at the pool made him want to see her again.

   (a) meeting   (b) fight   (c) swimming race

3. Eileen tried to sit *astride* the merry-go-round horse.

   (a) next to   (b) with both legs on one side   (c) with a leg on each side

4. Jeff *infuriated* Eileen when he pushed her into the pool.

   (a) made laugh   (b) made cry   (c) made angry

5. The loud barking made Jeff think that the dog was *ferocious*.

   (a) very large   (b) badly trained   (c) vicious

6. After taking off the dark glasses, Jeff saw the world with greater *clarity*.

   (a) sympathy   (b) clearness   (c) beauty

Bonus Activity: Decide which of the words in parentheses belongs in the sentence and write it in the answer blank.

7. Eileen wasn't sure what to _____ to the dance.   (ware, wear, where)

8. She said that _____ not going to the school dance.   (your, you're)

9. I hope that _____ okay with your parents if the dance ends late. (its, it's)

10. Do you know _____ parents are going to be able to drive us back and forth?   (whose, who's)

Homographs

(Keyed to "Blind Sunday" Pages 148–172)

When you look a word up in a dictionary, you may see two or more words with the same spelling. A small number is next to each word. In many dictionaries, the small numbers mean that even though the words have the same spellings, they come from different words and have different histories. Words like this are called **homographs.** You have to look at the different entries to find the meaning you are looking for.

Directions: Study the dictionary entries. Then circle the correct answer.

> **school¹** (skool) *noun* **1.** place for learning. **2.** building for teaching and learning. **3.** all the people in such a place: *The whole school was there.* [from Old English *scol,* from Latin *schola,* from Greek *schole,* meaning "leisure for study"]
>
> **school²** (skool) *noun* **1.** a large group of fish that swim together. —*verb* **2.** to move about, like a group of fish. [from a Dutch word meaning "group, crowd"]
>
> **tear¹** (tār) *verb* **tore, torn, tear·ing 1.** to pull apart by force; rip. **2.** to make a hole by ripping. **3.** to remove by pulling up. —*noun* **4.** the act of ripping. **5.** a torn place; a rip. [from Old English *teran,* meaning "to rip"]
>
> **tear²** (tēr) *noun* **1.** a drop of liquid that flows from the eye. **2.** anything shaped like such a drop. —*verb* **3.** to flow with liquid from the eyes. [from Old English *tear*]

1. Are *school¹* and *school²* pronounced the same way? **yes   no**

2. Are *tear¹* and *tear²* pronounced the same way? **yes   no**

3. Where would you find the meaning for a building with classrooms? **school¹   school²**

4. Which numbered definition gives you the meaning for a building with classrooms? **1 2 3**

5. If you are crying, which *tear* do you mean? **tear¹   tear²**

6. If you are talking about a school of fish, which *school* do you mean? **school¹   school²**

7. Which *tear* would rhyme with *fear*? **tear¹   tear²**

8. Which entry for *tear* would tell you about a rip? **tear¹   tear²**

9. Which *school* comes from a Dutch word? **school¹   school²**

10. Which *tear* would rhyme with *care*? **tear¹   tear²**

Word Mastery Exercise

(Keyed to "Staley Fleming's Hallucination" Pages 182–185)

Directions: Circle the letter of the word or phrase that best defines each of the words from "Staley Fleming's Hallucination" printed in *italics* below. Use the context of each word to help determine its meaning.

1. The doctor believed that the monster was probably a *hallucination*.

   (a) shadow on the wall   (b) cruel trick
   (c) something thought to have been seen that doesn't exist

2. He *recommended* a doctor who treated mental problems.

   (a) warned against   (b) suggested using   (c) brought along

3. The doctor had a *theory* about the death of Atwell Barton.

   (a) idea to explain   (b) incorrect idea   (c) wild idea

4. Was it just a *coincidence* that the dog howled when it did?

   (a) careful plan   (b) something accidentally happening at the same time
   (c) trick someone has been paid to play

5. The doctor *strode* across the room.

   (a) tiptoed   (b) ran quickly   (c) walked firmly

Bonus Activity: In a famous play, a woman named Mrs. Malaprop uses words incorrectly and accidentally says funny things. Incorrect words of the kind she used are now known as **malapropisms.** Each sentence below has a malapropism. Circle it, and on the blank next to the sentence, write the word you think was meant.

6. *Big* is a cinnamon for *large*. _____

7. Everything became as confusing as a three-ring circle. _____

8. We sang the national antonym before the game. _____

9. He couldn't sing because he had a straw throat. _____

10. My favorite dessert is a banana splint. _____

Fun with Puns

> A **pun** is a humorous play on words that are similar. One pun you may have heard is a riddle: "When is a door not a door?" The answer is, "When it's ajar." *Ajar* means "partly open," but the listener hears, "When it's *a jar*." Puns use homophones, homographs, and other similar words to create humor. Many people groan when they hear puns, but they still enjoy them.

Directions: For each pun below, figure out what the play on words is. Use a dictionary to help you if necessary.

1. Flip asked Flop, "Why did you take the rabbit to the barber?" Flop answered, "Because I wanted to get a *hare cut*."

    What similar words help make that pun?

    _____ and _____

    What does each mean? _____

    _____

2. After the fish market closed, there was only one live fish left. He was the *sole* survivor.

    What are the two meanings of *sole* that make that a pun?

    _____   _____

3. Some chickens wanted to act, but their comedy didn't make anyone laugh. Everybody called their work a *fowl* play.

    What similar words help make that pun?

    _____ and _____

    What does each mean? _____

    _____

4. Two dolphin trainers discussed why one rode a dolphin to the shore. "Was it by accident?" the first one asked. "No," said the second, "I did it on *porpoise*."

    What similar words help make that pun?

    _____ and _____

    What does each mean? _____

    _____

5. Write your own pun. If you cannot think of anything, here are some words that might help you think of an idea: bat, seal, heard/herd, bear/bare.

    _____

Using a Pronunciation Key

(Keyed to "Staley Fleming's Hallucination" Pages 182–185)

Pronunciations in *The Cornerstone Anthology* are shown by respelling words with regular letters of the alphabet. Dictionaries, however, show how to pronounce words by using symbols in addition to letters of the alphabet. Each dictionary has its own system of pronunciation. It gives you a *key* to help you figure out how to say each of the sounds.

Some words may have pronunciations that look exactly like the way the word is spelled; for example, *help* (help) and *bat* (bat). Most pronunciations, however, are noticeably different from the spelling of the word.

Many words have more than one syllable. Two kinds of marks are used in pronunciations to show which syllables have accents. The mark ′ is used to show the heavy accent in a word. The mark ″ is used to show a lighter accent. The pronunciation system used here shows the mark after the syllable. Many syllables do not have any accent.

Some words have different pronunciations for different parts of speech. For example, *conduct* is pronounced (kon′dukt) as a noun and (kən dukt′) as a verb.

---

af · ter · ward (af′tər wərd) *adverb* at a later time.

af · ter · word (af′tər wûrd″) *noun* a section at the end of a literary work.

beau (bō) *noun*, plural *beaus, beaux* (bōz) **1.** a boyfriend.

bed · room (bed′room″, -room″) *noun* a room for sleeping.

bough (bou) *noun* a large branch of a tree.

bow¹ (bou) *verb* **1.** to bend the knee or body.

bow² (bō) *noun* **1.** device made of wood for shooting arrows.

bow³ (bou) *noun* the forward end of a ship or airplane.

co · in · cide (kō″in sīd′) *verb* **1.** to happen in the same place or time.

co · in · ci · dence (ko in′si dəns) *noun* **1.** two or more events happening at the same time.

di · ag · nose (di′əg nōs″, -nōz″) *verb* **1.** to determine the cause of an illness.

di · ag · no · sis (di″əg nō′sis) *noun*, *plural* **-ses** (-sēz). **1.** determination of cause of illness.

dis · turb (di stûrb′) *verb* **1.** to interrupt rest or business.

fore · foot (fōr′foot″, fôr′-) *noun*, *plural* **-feet. 1.** the front foot of a four-legged animal.

glow (glō) *noun* **1.** a light sent out from something heated.

hal · lu · ci · na · tion (hə loo″s ə nā′shən) *noun* **1.** an imaginary thing seen or heard.

New · found · land (noo″ fənd land′) *noun* **1.** a large island.

ob · ject (*noun* ob′jikt, -jekt; *verb* əb jekt′)

pa · tient (pā′shənt) *noun* **1.** a person who is under medical care.

per · fect (*adjective & noun* pûr′fikt; *verb* pər fekt′)

pow · er (pou′ər) *noun* **1.** the ability to do or act; capability.

psy · chi · a · trist (sī kī′ ə trist, si-) *noun* a doctor who treats emotional disorders.

psy · chi · a · try (sī kī′ ə trē, si-) *noun* the practice of treating emotional disorders.

ran · dom (ran′dəm) *adjective* happening without definite aim.

shout (shout) *verb* **1.** to call or cry out loudly and strongly.

spe · cial · ist (spech′ ə list) *noun* **1.** a doctor devoted to a specific branch of medicine.

the · o · ry (thē′ə rē, ther′ē) *noun*, *plural* **-ries. 1.** explanation based on careful observation.

thou¹ (thou) *pronoun* **1.** an old word meaning "you."

thou² (thou) *noun*, *plural* **thous** *Slang* one thousand dollars.

though (thō) *conjunction* **1.** word used to introduce a subordinate.

thought (thot) *noun* **1.** the product of mental activity.

40 / THE CORNERSTONE ANTHOLOGY

Vowel Sounds

a	hat, act	oi	oil
ā	able, face	o͝o	book
â	care	o͞o	ooze, move
ä	art, palm	ou	out, house
e	ebb, let	u	up, cut
ē	equal, bee	û	urge
i	it, pin	ə =	a as in above
ī	ice, five		e as in taken
o	hot, rock		i as in pencil
ō	over, go		o as in lemon
ô	order		u as in circus

Consonant Sounds

b	but, rob	p	pup
ch	child, rich	r	run
d	did	s	sun, yes
f	fun, if	sh	she, wish
g	go, big	t	tot
h	he	th	thin
hw	which	t͟h	that
j	joy	v	very, have
k	king, seek	w	will
l	log, coal	y	yes
m	me, him	z	zer, fuzz
n	no, on	zh	measure
ng	song, ring		

Directions: Use the pronunciation key and the pronunciations on page 40 to answer the questions on this page. Circle the correct answer or answers.

1. Which syllable of *afterward* has the accent? **first   second   third**

2. Which of these words has both a heavy and light accent? **afterward   afterword**

3. Which of the following is pronounced the same as *beau?* **bow¹   bow²   bow³**

4. Which of the following is pronounced the same as *bough?* **bow¹   bow²   bow³**

5. Is the accent on the same syllable in *coincide* and *coincidence?* **yes   no**

6. How many correct pronunciations are shown for *diagnose?* **one   two   three**

7. What is the correct consonant sound at the end of *diagnose?* **/s/   /z/   either /s/ or /z/**

8. How many correct pronunciations are shown for *diagnosis?* **one   two   three**

9. Which sound is the /û/ sound in *disturb* the same as? **the *u* in *cut*   the *u* in *urge*   the *u* in *circus***

10. How many syllables are there in *hallucination?* **three   four   five   six**

11. In the pronunciation shown for *Newfoundland,* do you pronounce the middle syllable like the word *found?* **yes   no**

12. Is the noun *object* pronounced the same way as the verb *object?* **yes   no**

13. Which syllable of *perfect* would have a heavy accent if you said, "a perfect day"? **first   last**

14. Which syllable of *perfect* would have a heavy accent if you said, "I want to perfect this machine"? **first   last**

15. How do you pronounce the *p* at the beginning of *psychiatrist?* **/p/   /ps/   it is silent**

16. In which of the following is the *o* pronounced like the *o* of *random?* **hot   lemon   over   order**

17. Which of the following letters are *not* used by themselves in the pronunciation key? **c   g   j   k   q   s**

18. Are the *th* of *thou¹* and *thou²* pronounced the same way? **yes   no**

Word Mastery Exercise

(Keyed to "Perseus and Medusa" Pages 188–192)

Directions: Circle the letter of the word or phrase that best defines each of the words from "Perseus and Medusa" printed in *italics* below. Use the context of each word to help determine its meaning.

1. The monster was so *hideous* that all who saw her turned into stone.

   (a) extremely powerful   (b) horribly ugly   (c) hard to find

2. She kept living *serpents* in the cave.

   (a) dragons   (b) wild animals   (c) snakes

3. The king sent his daughter and grandson away because a *prophecy* said that the boy would one day kill the king.

   (a) witch   (b) warrior from another town   (c) warning about the future

4. Perseus went to Larissa to *compete* in the games.

   (a) take part in a contest   (b) write a story about   (c) kill somebody

5. The hero *plunged* a sword into the monster's body.

   (a) hid   (b) found   (c) jabbed

Bonus Activity: Writers often compare people to those in myths and legends. Figure out which name from the word box makes the best comparison for each idea and write it in the blank.

Andromeda	Athena	Hermes	Medusa	Perseus

6. as ugly as _____

7. as wise as _____

8. as brave as _____

9. as swift as _____

10. as beautiful as _____

Following Directions

(Keyed to "Perseus and Medusa" Pages 188–192)

If Perseus had not followed Athena's directions carefully, he might have been turned into stone. Be sure you read and follow the directions!

Directions: Read the whole page before you do any writing.

Name: _____ Date: _____

1. Circle all the words that have two syllables.
   cotton   flight   moor   litter   pickle   stout

2. Rewrite the words below in alphabetical order. Begin the first word with a capital letter. End the last word with a question mark.
   most   everyone   tires   fix   can   motorcycle

   _____

3. Draw a line through the word that is not an animal's name.
   walrus   elephant   snake   bush   lion

4. Write an *X* over the word that has the most letters.
   anniversary   peculiar   cabinet   context   synonym

5. Draw a line under the word that is first in alphabetical order.
   muffin   mouth   moon   maid   man

6. Write five words that rhyme with the word *bee.*

   _____

7. Draw a box around all the words that are written the same way backward and forward.
   did   was   saw   nun   bit   bib   pat   tap   pup

8. Draw a line above all the words that have an *r.*
   rug   pray   try   alarm   more   sauce   are

9. Write a check (√) next to all the words that describe something people wear.
   hat   shoes   pencil   belt   socks   paper

10. Cross out the names that were in the story "Perseus and Medusa."
    Athena   Diana   Perseus   Medusa   Zeus   Ariadne

11. Write only your name and the date at the top of the page. Ignore the directions in items 1–10. If you have followed the directions at the top of the page, you can now sit back and watch your classmates at work.

Word Mastery Exercise

Directions: Circle the letter of the word or phrase that best defines each of the words from "Theseus and the Minotaur" printed in *italics* below. Use the context of each word to help determine its meaning.

1. A *labyrinth* is

   (a) a king's palace.   (b) an arena for games.   (c) a place with many winding paths.

2. An *architect*

   (a) designs buildings.   (b) guards bulls.   (c) works for a king.

3. Someone who *devours* a meal

   (a) just picks at it.   (b) eats it quickly.   (c) cooks for others.

4. People are said to be in *mourning* when

   (a) the sun rises.   (b) someone has died.   (c) danger is near.

5. The *Minotaur* was a monster with

   (a) snakes in its hair.   (b) a lion's body.   (c) a bull's head.

Bonus Activity: Choose the correct spelling from each pair of words and write the word in the answer blank.

6. The thought of his son's death was more than Aegeus could _____.
   (bare, bear)

7. He _____ himself into the sea.   (threw, through)

8. Theseus promised to lower the black _____ if he returned safely.
   (sail, sale)

9. Theseus managed to find the _____ spot in the monster's neck.
   (weak, week)

10. Theseus _____ the battle with the Minotaur.   (one, won)

Personification

(Keyed to "Theseus and the Minotaur" Pages 195–199)

> To make writing come alive, writers often give human qualities to things or ideas. Giving nonhuman things human qualities is called *personification*. Here are some examples of personification:
> Love walked in the door. (Love is an idea; it cannot walk.)
> The tree raised its arms to the sky. (Trees do not have arms; people do.)

Directions: Read each sentence below and decide what human quality each idea or thing has. Write an explanation on the blank. The first one has been done for you.

1. The wind cried at the door, asking to be let in.

   The wind is given the human attribute of speech.

2. Freedom gathered people to her side.

   _____

3. The stars in the sky winked at us and invited us to reach high.

   _____

4. Hunger laughed in the faces of the weary people.

   _____

5. Honor called us to battle.

   _____

6. Fate was always playing tricks on us.

   _____

7. The rocks complained of the rough soldiers' boots.

   _____

8. The small voice of Hope cheered us when everything seemed lost.

   _____

Bonus Activity: Write your own example of personification.

_____

Word Mastery Exercise

Directions: Circle the letter of the word or phrase that best defines each of the words from "The Open Window" printed in *italics* below. Use the context of each word to help determine its meaning.

1. The Sappleton family *endeavored* to be polite to Mr. Nuttel.

   (a) stopped   (b) refused   (c) tried

2. Framton's sister was afraid that he would never leave his country *retreat*.

   (a) quiet place for rest   (b) hospital for very sick people
   (c) hotel with many amusements

3. Instead of trying to be friendly, he often sat around *moping*.

   (a) insulting others   (b) yelling   (c) being sad and quiet

4. He like to hunt in the *moor*.

   (a) lake   (b) wild, open land   (c) jungle

5. The *bog* could be a dangerous place, especially in wet weather.

   (a) road   (b) lake   (c) marsh

6. Her voice *faltered* as she spoke of the missing men.

   (a) grew hoarse   (b) seemed unsteady   (c) was bitter

7. Framton thought that the story was too *ghastly*, and he changed the subject.

   (a) horrible   (b) personal   (c) unbelievable

8. He seemed to be *constantly* talking about his health and his doctors.

   (a) cheerfully   (b) without stopping   (c) afraid to be

9. The frightened man made a *headlong* dash out of the house.

   (a) fast, without thinking   (b) falling on his head   (c) carefully planned

10. Vera's *specialty* was making up wild stories.

    (a) thing not liked   (b) thing done well   (c) thing feared

Bonus Activity: Use at least two of the words above to write a description of one of the characters in the story. Do your writing on a separate piece of paper.

Compare and Contrast

(Keyed to "The Open Window" Pages 207–211)

> A **comparison** tells how things are alike. A **contrast** shows how they are different.

Directions: Tell whether each statement below is a comparison or a contrast. Circle the correct answer.

1. Vera was very attractive, like her aunt. **Comparison   Contrast**

2. Vera found it easy to talk to people. Framton, on the other hand, found conversation difficult. **Comparison   Contrast**

3. The day was bright and sunny, like a perfect summer day. **Comparison   Contrast**

4. The dogs were as wet and dirty as the men who came in with them. **Comparison   Contrast**

5. Framton thought his health was an interesting subject, while the others found it boring. **Comparison   Contrast**

6. She was as bright and cheerful as a spring day. **Comparison   Contrast**

7. He was as nervous as they were calm. **Comparison   Contrast**

8. Vera seemed like an ordinary young girl, but her stories were wild and definitely not ordinary. **Comparison   Contrast**

9. The story of Saki's life is as romantic and exciting as his fiction. **Comparison   Contrast**

10. The strange story of the men's disappearance did not seem to fit this rather ordinary house. **Comparison   Contrast**

11. Mr. Sappleton enjoyed singing. His wife did not. **Comparison   Contrast**

12. The story Vera told about the wild dogs shocked everyone. The truth would have been boring. **Comparison   Contrast**

Bonus Activity: Write one comparison and one contrast based on "The Open Window."

_____

_____

Summarizing

(Keyed to "The Open Window" Pages 207–211)

A **summary** tells the most important points in a short form. It leaves out details of little importance and just gives the main idea. For example, a summary of "The Open Window" might be:

Framton Nuttel visits the Sappleton house and Vera tells him that Mr. Sappleton and his brothers-in-law disappeared three years ago. Her aunt, she says, is still waiting for their return. Mrs. Sappleton enters and watches the window for the returning men. Three figures appear in the twilight, and Framton runs away terrified. Vera has really made up the story of the disappearance.

Directions: Choose three of the stories listed below and write a short summary of each.

Mama and Papa
Thicker Than Water
Cinderella

Prairie Fire
The Confidence Game
The Three Bears

Shoes for Hector
Perseus and Medusa
Goldilocks

1. Story (*title*)/Summary: _____

_____

_____

_____

_____

2. Story (*title*)/Summary: _____

_____

_____

_____

_____

3. Story (*title*)/Summary: _____

_____

_____

_____

_____

Word Mastery Exercise

(Keyed to "The Ten-Armed Monster of Newfoundland" Pages 220–226)

Directions: Circle the letter of the word or phrase that best defines each of the words from "The Ten-Armed Monster of New-foundland" printed in *italics* below. Use the context of each word to help determine its meaning.

1. Most people *regarded* the tales of the kraken as make-believe.

    (a) considered   (b) watched over   (c) disliked

2. The *legendary* Vikings fought sea monsters and were ten feet tall.

    (a) honest   (b) walking with big steps   (c) found in legends

3. At first, the thing in the water was just a dark *blob*.

    (a) shiny creature   (b) shapeless thing   (c) ink squirter

4. The men and boy *shuddered* as the creature reached toward them.

    (a) cried out   (b) trembled   (c) fought back

5. A dark rain cloud *hovered* above them.

    (a) hung in the air   (b) moved quickly   (c) poured down

6. Tom's father looked at the puddle beneath his feet and started to *bail* out the boat.

    (a) dip water out of   (b) unload objects from   (c) plug up holes

7. As the monster attacked, Tom *wheeled* around to strike back.

    (a) moved on skates   (b) grabbed an oar   (c) turned quickly

8. The monster's arm seemed to *correspond* to the arm of a small squid.

    (a) match   (b) write   (c) be more powerful than

9. Tom was *far-sighted* enough to keep proof that the monster was real.

    (a) stubborn   (b) in need of glasses   (c) able to look ahead

10. The squid's arms *slithered* onto the boat.

    (a) slapped   (b) moved unevenly   (c) moved like a snake

Bonus Activity: Use a dictionary to find several different meanings for the word *bail*. Write two meanings below.

bail: _____

bail: _____

Matching the Picture to the Description

(Keyed to "The Ten-Armed Monster of Newfoundland" Pages 220–226)

There are many real animals that are unknown to most people in the world. Would you know them if you saw them? Would you be able to visualize them if you read a description of them?

1. _____

2. _____

3. _____

4. _____

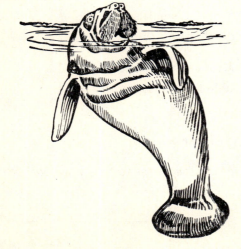

5. _____

6. _____

Directions: Match the paragraph that describes the animal to the picture of the animal on page 50. Write the name of the animal under its picture.

Dugong   A dugong is a mammal that lives in the sea. It has long flippers instead of front legs. Its tail flipper is sharply pointed at the two ends. Dugongs are usually brownish or grayish in color. They have stiff hair around the mouth. Dugongs stay under water for up to ten minutes at a time. Then they must come to the surface to breathe. Another name for a dugong is a sea cow.

Orca   An orca is a mammal that lives in the ocean. It has flippers instead of front legs, and a fin sticking up from the back. Instead of back legs, it has a kind of curved flipper called a fluke. An orca has a rounded snout, a white patch above each eye, a black upper body, and a white lower body. An orca breathes through a hole at the top of the head and must come to the surface to breathe. Orcas are also known as killer whales, but they are really a kind of dolphin.

Sea Otter   A sea otter is a water-loving mammal that spends most of its time in the ocean. It has a large, rounded head and short legs. The back feet are webbed, and sometimes look like broad flippers. Sea otters like to swim and float on their backs. They eat many kinds of shellfish, often resting their food on their chests while floating. Their teeth are strong and can crack the shells of most of their favorite foods.

Mongoose   A mongoose can be a snake's worst enemy, since snakes are among the mongoose's favorite foods. Even though a poisonous snake can kill a mongoose, most mongooses are too quick to be bitten by a snake. A mongoose is a furry animal with a pointed head and a long, thin, furry tail. The tail is often longer than the mongoose's head and body combined. Although mongooses come in many different colors, they are all usually lighter in color on the under side.

Genet   A genet is a gray or yellow animal with brown or black spots. It has a pointed snout, round ears, large eyes, and whiskers. Genets usually hunt at night and spend their days in protected places such as hollow trees or cracks in rocks. They have very short legs and a long, narrow body. Their tails have black and white rings. When they move along the ground, their bodies seem to grow longer. A genet can get through any opening that is large enough for its head.

Lesser Panda   A lesser panda looks more like a raccoon than a great panda. It has dark patches around the eyes and rings on the tail. Its body is a reddish brown, but it has white areas around the mouth, cheeks, and ears. The lesser panda eats mostly vegetables, but sometimes it eats eggs and small animals. Lesser pandas are active mostly at night, and spend their days sleeping in trees. They are found only in Asia.

Word Mastery Exercise

(Keyed to "Prone" Pages 231–240)

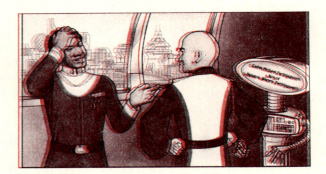

Directions: Circle the letter of the word or phrase that best defines each of the words from "Prone" printed in *italics* below. Use the context of each word to help determine its meaning.

1. The General had the *impression* that something strange was taking place.

   (a) scared feeling
   (b) written warning
   (c) unclear idea

2. Even though equipment was destroyed, it was clear that there had been no *sabotage*.

   (a) destroying property on purpose
   (b) loss of military guns and ammunition
   (c) soldiers' lives lost

3. The commander wanted to hand in his *resignation* because of the terrible events taking place.

   (a) complaints about military system
   (b) request for a promotion
   (c) notice that he was quitting

4. It was *evident* that the events taking place had no reasonable explanation.

   (a) very clear   (b) hard to believe   (c) proved in court

5. Mitchie seemed to be an *extreme* example of a person who was accident-prone.

   (a) foolish   (b) greater than usual   (c) easy to see

6. The door struck the lieutenant and injured his bones and *cartilage*.

   (a) blood vessels   (b) leg muscles   (c) soft bone parts

7. The lieutenant *winced* as he was struck, but he didn't scream.

   (a) drew back in pain   (b) moaned softly   (c) fell in a faint

8. Mitchie *woefully* explained his problem to the SupCom.

   (a) in great detail   (b) sadly   (c) without emotion

9. The SupCom expected that Mitchie's presence on Mars would do *considerable* damage to Terra's enemy.

   (a) well-planned   (b) a small amount of   (c) fairly great

10. Mitchie alone would be enough to make up an *occupation* force in Mars.

    (a) military attack   (b) controlling an enemy territory
    (c) setting up business firms

Determining Time Order

(Keyed to "Prone" Pages 231–240)

Directions: The following groups of sentences are not in the correct time order. Read the sentences in each group carefully to see which sentence should go first, second, third, fourth, and last. Use the clue words, such as *first, next, later,* and *at last,* to help you figure out the order of events. Label them *1, 2, 3, 4, 5* to show their correct order.

A.

_____ (a) After he heard what Jeremy's mother said, the police chief scratched his head.

_____ (b) Then Jeremy, a five-year-old, became the first human to meet an alien.

_____ (c) Finally the police chief decided that it was just another crank call and he paid no attention to it.

_____ (d) When his mother realized that Jeremy's friend was not human, she called the police.

_____ (e) In the beginning, the aliens landed so quietly that nobody knew they were there.

B.

_____ (a) At last, the combined Earth forces were able to drive away the Martians and to take back control of their own planet.

_____ (b) So the Earth people decided to forget the disagreements between countries and put all their strength into fighting a common enemy.

_____ (c) Then the Earth people decided that if they did not join together to fight back, the whole planet would be ruled by Mars.

_____ (d) Before people knew what was happening, one quarter of Earth was threatened by Martians.

_____ (e) When the Martians first attacked Earth, Earth people weren't prepared for the attack.

C.

_____ (a) Last week, Mercedes found a small gold coin in the street.

_____ (b) After checking everything else, she realized that the coin on her dresser was sending out a message in a secret code.

_____ (c) So she put it on her dresser and left it there.

_____ (d) Yesterday, she heard a strange beeping noise coming from her dresser.

_____ (e) When she got home, she looked in her book of foreign coins, but she could not find a picture of the coin she had found.

Understanding Spatial Order

(Keyed to "Prone" Pages 231–240)

In reading, it is sometimes important to understand the order of things in space—where they appear in relationship to one another. Sometimes a drawing is included to help you understand the order. At other times, you must figure out the space order by following clues within the story. Some clue words that will help you understand space order are *next to, closer, farther,* and *farthest away.*

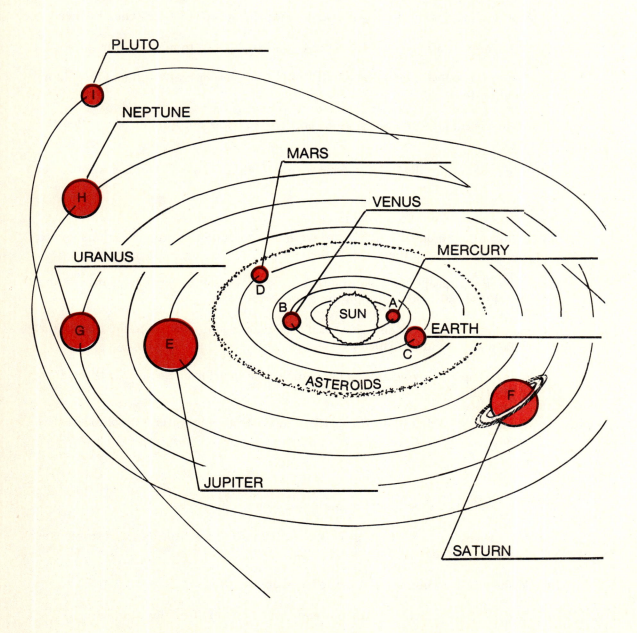

PLUTO

NEPTUNE

MARS

VENUS

MERCURY

URANUS

EARTH

ASTEROIDS

JUPITER

SATURN

SUN

A. Directions: Use the paragraphs below to help you figure out which planet is which in the drawing on page 54. Label the planets in the drawing by writing their names on the lines next to them.

Earth, the planet on which we live, is the third planet from the sun. Mercury is the planet closest to the sun. Between Mercury and Earth is the planet Venus, a planet about which we know very little. After Earth, the planet next farthest from the sun is Mars, which has been visited by unmanned spaceships from Earth. These four planets are often called the inner planets. Just past the inner planets is a ring of thousands of tiny asteroids, which are too small to be considered true planets.

Of the five outer planets, Jupiter is the closest to the sun. After Jupiter comes Saturn and then Uranus. The last two planets change places as eighth and ninth from the sun. Although Pluto travels the farthest from the sun, it is not always the planet that is most distant from the sun. That is because Pluto's path sometimes crosses the path of Neptune, which is usually the eighth farthest from the sun. When Pluto is closer than Neptune, Neptune becomes the farthest planet from the sun.

B. Directions: Answer the questions below. Write the correct answers on the blanks.

1. Which two planets are closest to Earth? _____ and

   _____

2. Which two planets are closest to the asteroids? _____ and

   _____

3. Which two planets change places as eighth and ninth from the sun? _____

   and _____

4. Is Saturn or Uranus closer to Jupiter? _____

5. Which of the inner planets is farthest from the sun? _____

Word Mastery Exercise

Directions: Circle the letter of the word or phrase that best defines each of the words from "My Hero" printed in *italics* below. Use the context of each word to help determine its meaning.

1. Jackson ran toward his dog, then *flinched* when he saw the grizzly bear chasing her.

   (a) drew back   (b) ran away
   (c) called for help

2. There was no time to *retrieve* his keys from the car trunk.

   (a) unlock   (b) go and bring back
   (c) search inside for

3. He hoped that the bear was a *sprinter*, not a long-distance runner.

   (a) one who cannot pick up speed   (b) one who falls easily
   (c) one who runs quickly just for short distances

4. If he fell with the bear so close behind him, he would be a *goner*.

   (a) one who cannot be saved   (b) one whose injury causes pain
   (c) one who mysteriously disappears

5. He tried to *scramble* up the rocky hill.

   (a) get someone confused   (b) walk carefully   (c) climb on hands and knees

6. It was foolish for the dog to *antagonize* the grizzly bear.

   (a) bark loudly at   (b) to annoy and make an enemy of   (c) follow the tracks of

7. Jackson *sheepishly* thanked the rancher for saving him.

   (a) in an embarrassed way   (b) by shaking his hand   (c) without saying a word

8. The grizzly's *bulk* kept him from moving quickly.

   (a) short legs   (b) injured paw   (c) large body

Bonus Activity: Can you figure out the meanings of the following words, which were made by adding suffixes to the base word *retrieve*? Use a dictionary to help you. Then write the meanings next to the words.

retrieval: _____

retriever: _____

Making Inferences

(Keyed to "My Hero" Pages 248–252)

When reading "My Hero" you have to make inferences to understand some parts of the story. Making inferences is part of understanding what we read, hear, and see. If you don't remember what an inference is, check the Glossary of Terms on pages 394–395.

Directions: Read each of the following statements about the story and make an inference about what has just happened. Answer the questions in your own words.

1. When the story begins, Jackson is throwing a tire iron and a jack into the trunk of the car. What has Jackson been doing?

   _____

2. When Jackson gets into the car, he reaches for the ignition switch. Then he realizes that he has left the ignition key in the trunk. What had Jackson meant to do when he got into the car?

   _____

3. When Jackson begins to climb the tree, the bear starts following him. What had Jackson hoped to do by climbing the tree?

   _____

4. The sound of the rifle shot scares the bear away. Did the rancher think it was necessary to kill the bear?

   _____

5. The rancher tells Jackson that he should get another dog. What does Jackson think the rancher means about his dog Detta?

   _____

6. The rancher says that two dogs protect each other. Each can get on one side of a bear. What does the rancher really mean about getting two dogs?

   _____

7. The rancher calls Jackson "son" and "young fella." What does that tell you about the ages of Jackson and the rancher?

   _____

8. The rancher says that people who live nearby never go into the woods with just one dog. He says you never know when she might turn out to be a retriever. What two meanings of the word *retriever* make his statement a pun?

   _____

Word Mastery Exercise

(Keyed to "Ooka and the Stolen Smell" Pages 255–257)

Directions: Circle the letter of the word or phrase that best defines each of the words from "Ooka and the Stolen Smell" printed in *italics* below. Use the context of each word to help determine its meaning.

1. Ooka, the judge, was known for his great *wit* in deciding cases.

    (a) humor   (b) intelligence   (c) unfairness

2. The young student was very *likable,* but also very poor.

    (a) hard to like   (b) easy to like   (c) quick to like others

3. The city *magistrate* agreed to hear the strange Case of the Stolen Smell.

    (a) police chief   (b) mayor   (c) judge

4. Ooka decided that the student was *obviously* guilty.

    (a) clearly   (b) probably   (c) not at all

5. The judge believed that *virtue* should be rewarded and crime punished.

    (a) catching criminals   (b) wealth   (c) goodness

6. Ooka believed that justice *prevailed* in his courtroom.

    (a) won out   (b) was hard to decide   (c) was not involved

7. The judge listened *gravely* to the evidence the shopkeeper presented.

    (a) although he was sick   (b) in a serious manner   (c) without paying attention

8. The *clink* of the student's coins was thought to be a fair payment for stealing the smell of the food.

    (a) sharp, metal sound   (b) small purse   (c) hidden supply

Bonus Activity: Choose any two words in *italics* above and write a sentence using each.

_____

_____

Distinguishing Sensory Images

(Keyed to "Ooka and the Stolen Smell" Pages 255–257)

Sounds and smells play an important part in "Ooka and the Stolen Smell." Sounds and smells are part of what we sense through the **five senses:** sight, smell, sound, taste, and touch. Writers often suggest the five senses to make their work more real.

Directions: Decide which one of the five senses each of the following sentences suggests. Write the name of the sense on the answer blank.

sight	smell	sound	taste	touch

_____ 1. The money felt hard and cold in his hand.

_____ 2. The tinkling wind chimes let him know that he was approaching the house.

_____ 3. Dinner was cooking, and her nose told her that there would be spaghetti sauce.

_____ 4. The bright, golden light streaming through the window woke her in the morning.

_____ 5. The lemon was tart on her tongue, but it was a nice change from the sweet sugar.

_____ 6. The buzzing of the alarm clock woke him to another day.

_____ 7. He enjoyed the spicy tacos and hot chili peppers.

_____ 8. A strange shape came toward them in the fog.

_____ 9. All day her clothes felt damp and cold.

_____ 10. A trace of perfume remained in the room long after the woman had left.

_____ 11. The sharp rocks scraped and scratched his bare feet.

_____ 12. Before long he could tell one bird's song from another.

_____ 13. The red, white, and blue balloons hung on the walls.,

_____ 14. Though decorated for a party, their noses told them that this was the school gym.

_____ 15. The guitar and bass played exciting rhythms and a spirited melody.

Identifying Elements of a Short Story

(Keyed to "Ooka and the Stolen Smell" Pages 255–257)

By now, you should know the most important ideas about a short story:

Character	Setting	Plot	Topic	Theme

Directions: Decide which of the five ideas above best describes each of the following. Then write the word on the answer blank.

1. _____

He was tall and quite thin. His face was lined and rough, as if he had been through difficult times. Although the corners of his mouth were turned down, there was a twinkle in his eyes as he spoke. His way of speaking suggested that he had once had a better life than his clothing indicated.

2. _____

The car screeched to a halt and two men in dark clothes got out. They ran toward the store just as a younger man was racing out. "Stop!" they shouted, but the young man ducked quickly down an alley. The men chased after him.

3. _____

A Day in School

4. _____

The streets were lined with tall buildings. Litter from a parade remained on the ground. Torn posters hung from buildings and lampposts. The evening softened the sight of the dirt and litter, and a child's eye caught the lighted windows that dotted the upper air.

5. _____

Anybody who wants to be a good athlete must spend a lot of time practicing.

6. _____

The sights, smells, and sounds in the streets of Tokyo were different from those of any city she had been in before. The words on shops were in Japanese characters. She couldn't understand the rapid talk going on around her. And the traffic moved differently from the traffic at home.

7. _____

Traveling in Other Countries

8. _____

Mrs. Miller had a reputation of being kind to people in trouble. When she first saw Tracy, Mrs. Miller gave her a big hug and asked if she were hungry. Only after she gave Tracy something to eat did she begin to try to find out how she could help her. Mrs. Miller had helped many young people, and Tracy knew that she could trust her.

9. _____

As he hit the baseball, he realized that it would go straight for the old man's window. The old man came out shouting and threatening to call the police. The boy tried to explain that it was an accident and that he would pay for the broken window, but the man wouldn't listen. He just kept screaming until everybody in the neighborhood came out to see what was happening.

10. _____

It is important to take time to listen to what others are saying.

11. _____

My Favorite Vacation

12. _____

The judge was known to take cases that no other judge would dream of taking. He understood that people wanted their day in court, so he was willing to listen to their petty fights. He believed that if he allowed them to deal with their problems by bringing their cases to court, he might be able to prevent more serious fights. He believed that he could do something to keep order in the city. That, he thought, made his life important.

13. _____

The stagecoach creaked over muddy roads and dusty lanes. Outside, the scenery changed as the coach wheeled by. Inside, the cabin was too small for the five people and their baggage. The air seemed hot and stale no matter what it was like outside. Every bump in the road could be felt; every sharp turn alarmed the passengers.

14. _____

She swam toward the shore, but the waves kept forcing her back. As time passed and she saw she was getting no closer, she realized she was getting more and more tired. Suddenly, she felt something push her from below. It began to maneuver her toward the shore. Almost afraid to look, she turned and realized it was a dolphin, a friendly dolphin who realized she needed help. Before long, she was close to the shore. "Thanks!" she called out, as the dolphin returned to the sea.

15. _____

Helpful Animals

Word Mastery Exercise

(Keyed to "The Kick" Pages 268–273)

Directions: Circle the letter of the word or phrase that best defines each of the words from "The Kick" printed in *italics* below. Use the context of each word to help determine its meaning.

1. His long legs gave him an *advantage* in winning a race.

    (a) cause of difficulty   (b) something that helps   (c) place to stand

2. It was hard to get anyone to *acknowledge* the fact that she was becoming a fast runner.

    (a) admit as true   (b) refuse to believe   (c) try to prove

3. A strong feeling of *competitiveness* kept her racing in spite of the difficulties.

    (a) stubborn ideas   (b) completeness   (c) trying to win

4. At the end of the race, her heart was beating and her mouth was *parched*.

    (a) very dry   (b) shouting   (c) drooling

5. She *concentrated* on reaching the finish line.

    (a) fell short   (b) gave all attention to   (c) thought little of

Bonus Activity: The word *kick* has many meanings. Decide which of the meanings below fits each sentence and write the letter of the meaning on the blank next to the sentence.

_____ 6. She gave him a *kick* to warn him to be quiet.

_____ 7. Watch out for the mule; it *kicks*.

_____ 8. The swimming instructor explained that the *kick* used in the sidestroke is different from the crawl.

_____ 9. He *kicked* the ball hard and hurt his toe.

_____ 10. She hoped that she would have enough energy for the *kick* as she ran toward the finish line.

(a) to strike with the foot

(b) to be in the habit of striking things with the foot

(c) last hard run at the finish line

(d) a blow with the foot

(e) a special motion made by the foot, as in swimming

Recognizing the Author's Purpose

(Keyed to "The Kick" Pages 268–273)

Most authors write for a purpose. The usual purposes are:

A. to entertain the reader
B. to try to make the reader agree with the author
C. to explain or teach something

Directions: Decide which purpose each of the following has. Then write *A*, *B*, or *C* on the answer blank.

_____ 1. a booklet on why smoking is bad for you

_____ 2. a funny story about a clown

_____ 3. a recipe telling how to make scrambled eggs

_____ 4. a videotape telling what to do in an emergency

_____ 5. an ad encouraging you to vacation in Florida

_____ 6. an adventure series on television

_____ 7. a movie about a space adventure

_____ 8. a science textbook about space

_____ 9. an article saying why the country should send rockets into space

_____ 10. a letter telling why there won't be a Valentine's dance this year

_____ 11. a letter to a newspaper giving reasons for spending more money on schools

_____ 12. a story about a boy and girl who fall in love

_____ 13. a book telling how to build a windmill

_____ 14. a book about the U. S. Constitution

_____ 15. an essay telling why we should love our country

_____ 16. a pamphlet explaining first-aid procedures

_____ 17. a newspaper editorial arguing for stricter laws for petty criminals

_____ 18. a caption for a cartoon

_____ 19. a set of directions for building a bookcase

_____ 20. a book of humorous poems

Word Mastery Exercise

Directions: Circle the letter of the word or phrase that best defines each of the words from "Dear Lovey Hart, I Am Desperate" printed in *italics* below. Use the context of each word to help determine its meaning.

1. Carrie had the *potential* for being a good reporter.

   (a) work already done   (b) newspaper job   (c) ability not yet used

2. She was *inspired* to write a column for the school paper.

   (a) filled with the spirit   (b) unwilling to help   (c) stuck with a job

3. To get information for stories, Carrie had to stay on *cordial* terms with students, teachers, and people in town.

   (a) friendly   (b) using first names   (c) business

4. Carrie's father thought that a teacher should have the right to *censor* stories written for the newspaper.

   (a) read and enjoy   (b) refuse to allow to be printed   (c) discuss with the writer

5. The students *resented* being treated as if they didn't know what they were doing.

   (a) sent letters to people about   (b) started a protest about   (c) had angry feelings about

6. Carrie told one student to try to make friends out of *acquaintances*.

   (a) former enemies   (b) people on the same team   (c) people you don't know well

Bonus Activity: Can you find the mistakes in the letter below? The mistakes may be in spelling, punctuation, or use of a word. Cross out each mistake and write the correction above it.

```
Dear Lovey Hart:

    I don't know how to begin talking to a boy
I like. Every time I sea him, I have trouble
thinking of what to say. My hands get sweaty
and my mouth gets patched.

    Can you give me any advise? I am desperit.

                              Yours truly,

                              Lovelorn
```

Writing a Business Letter

(Keyed to "Dear Lovey Hart, I Am Desperate" Pages 276–281)

People often have to write business letters. A business letter is set up in a special way. These are the parts of a business letter:

                                              Your Street Address
                                              Your City, State   Zip Code
                                              Date

Name of Company or Person
Company's Street Address
City, State   Zip Code

Dear (name or title):

(Your message, written in paragraphs, goes here.)

                                              Yours truly,

                                              Your name

Directions: Write a letter to the president of the XYZ Television Station at 234 Video Drive in your city. Tell why the company should not take your favorite television show off the air. Mention the show by name and give two reasons you like it. Use your own address or the address of your school and today's date.

_____

_____

_____

_____

_____

_____

_____

_____

_____

Reading a Pie Graph

(Keyed to "Dear Lovey Hart, I Am Desperate" Pages 276–281)

A **pie graph** is a circle-shaped graph that shows how a whole amount is divided into parts. Think of a pie graph as an actual pie. Then you can see how big a piece of the pie is shown by each part.

Federal Money for Public Education, 1984
Total Amount, $17,044,773,000

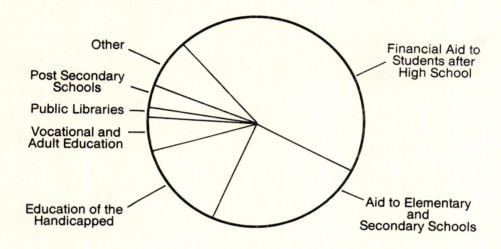

Directions: Use the pie graph above to answer the questions below. Write your answers on the blanks.

1. What was the largest amount of federal aid set aside for?

   _____

2. Was this amount more or less than half of the total?

   _____

3. What was about one fourth of the entire amount of federal aid set aside for?

   _____

4. Was more money set aside for educating the handicapped or for vocational and adult education?

   _____

5. According to the pie graph, what was the smallest share of the total set aside for?

   _____

Word Mastery Exercise

(Keyed to "The Wolf of Thunder Mountain" Pages 285–292)

Directions: Circle the letter of the word or phrase that best defines each of the words from "The Wolf of Thunder Mountain" printed in *italics* below. Use the context of each word to help determine its meaning.

1. Grandpa believed that the wolf was growing a *mite* smarter each year.

    (a) little bit   (b) whole lot   (c) somewhat less

2. The boy's mother thought that Grandpa was getting *puny* as he grew old.

    (a) forgetful   (b) bad-tempered   (c) weak

3. The wolf *bounded* out of the trap and into the woods.

    (a) was tied up   (b) leaped   (c) wiggled

4. The boy *strained* his ears to hear the wolf's footsteps.

    (a) made to work hard   (b) scratched   (c) used a pot to help

5. By Grandpa's *reckoning,* the wolf had a right to live free in the woods.

    (a) way of thinking   (b) spoiling things for others   (c) special feeling for wild animals

6. Grandpa's ability to think like a wolf gave him an *advantage* in dealing with the wolf.

    (a) special trouble   (b) something that helps   (c) no extra help

7. The boy *braced* his arm against the tree to keep the gun steady enough to shoot.

    (a) held firm   (b) tied   (c) scraped

8. The boy was surprised when Grandpa asked him to *spring* the trap.

    (a) set up to work   (b) place in position   (c) open so it can't work

Bonus Activity: Think of two different meanings for the word *spring*. Write a sentence for each meaning. Do not use the meaning in number 8, above.

_____

_____

Using Research Skills

(Keyed to "The Wolf of Thunder Mountain" Pages 285–292)

> When you have to find out information, a library is usually the best place to go. You may need to use **reference** books, such as dictionaries, encyclopedias, almanacs, and atlases. You may also need to use the library's card catalog.
> Below is a list of some of the reference sources that you can find in a library. Read the description of each. Then answer the questions on page 69.

Directions: A dictionary gives the meanings of words. It also tells how to pronounce words, including the names of some people and places. If you do not know the plural of a word, or if you don't know whether it begins with a capital letter, you can find out in a dictionary. Many dictionaries also give the histories of words, telling where they come from.

Encyclopedia: An encyclopedia has basic information on many subjects. Often, an encyclopedia is a good place to begin your research on a subject. Encyclopedias tell about plants, animals, people, places, ideas, and things, and where they are found. It usually has maps and pictures. The information in most encyclopedias is in alphabetical order. Most encyclopedias are made up of many books, called *volumes.* To find the volume you need, you can look in the volume beginning with the same letter of the alphabet as your subject, or you can look in the *index,* which is often the last volume of the encyclopedia.

Atlas: An atlas is a book of maps. Most atlases have maps of every part of the world. Some maps show whole continents of the world, such as Asia or Africa. Other maps show countries, states, or even just cities. In some atlases you may find maps showing how much it rains and what the average temperature is in a certain area. Other maps may show what the population is in different parts of the world. If you want to find a place in an atlas, look in the index at the back for the page number to turn to. Most atlases also give a number and letter to help you find a certain place on a page. That is very much like the system for using the map on pages 12–13 of this workbook.

Almanac: An almanac has lists of many kinds of information. Since most almanacs are published each year, a recent almanac often provides more up-to-date information than other reference books. You can find lists of Presidents of the United States in an almanac. You can find the population of states, cities, and countries. You can find out the names of winning sports teams, award-winning plays and movies, postage rates for sending mail, and the names of your senators and representatives. To find out which page to turn to, use the index. In some almanacs, the index is at the front of the book.

Card Catalog: The card catalog in your library is like a very large index. It tells you the names of the books in your library. There are three kinds of cards. *Subject* cards help you find the authors and titles of books on a particular subject. The subject is at the top of a subject card. *Author* cards help you find books written by a particular author. The author's name is also at the top of an author card. *Title* cards help you find a book if you know the title, but do not know who wrote it.

Directions: Decide which of the following would be most useful in helping you find the information you need. Write the answer on the blank. (In some cases, there will be more than one correct answer.)

almanac   atlas   card catalog   dictionary   encyclopedia

1. What is the plural of *wolf?* _____

2. Does the state of Montana border on Canada? _____ or _____

3. Who is the governor of South Dakota? _____

4. Does the library have any books about wolves? _____

5. Where are wolves found? _____

6. What does the word *Chippewa* mean? _____

7. Who won the World Series in 1985? _____

8. Which books by Paul Lawrence Dunbar are in the library? _____

9. Where in the state of North Dakota is the city of Minot? _____

10. How do you pronounce *Minot?* _____

11. What are some basic facts about North Dakota? _____ or _____

12. Which states touch the Pacific Ocean? _____

13. Which Canadian provinces touch the Arctic Ocean? _____

14. Who is the Prime Minister of Canada? _____

15. What is the most recent figure for the population of Idaho? _____

16. Who wrote *Call of the Wild?* _____

17. Who won the Academy Award for best actress in 1956? _____

18. Which islands in the Pacific Ocean are nearest to Hawaii? _____

19. How is maple syrup made? _____

20. Who was Alfred Nobel and what did he invent? _____

Bonus Activity: Choose any one question above and answer it. Next to the answer, write where you found the information.

21. _____

_____

Recognizing Cause and Effect

(Keyed to "The Wolf of Thunder Mountain" Pages 285–292)

Most stories have cause-and-effect situations. Understanding the cause and its effect helps us understand the story. Clue words such as *since, because, so,* and *for that reason* help us.

Directions: In each sentence below, decide which is the cause and which is the effect. Draw one line under the cause. Draw two lines under the effect. Circle the clue words that help us figure out the cause and effect. The first one has been done for you.

1. The lumberjacks went inside the store because they heard Grandpa coming down the street.

2. Since a car could not swim across a river, Grandpa used a horse to travel.

3. The boy's mother thought that Grandpa was getting old and weak, so she expected him to move to town.

4. The she-wolf was following Grandpa, so he had to kill her.

5. The wolf was not caught in the trap; for that reason he ran off when Grandpa prepared to shoot.

6. The wolf wanted to remember Grandpa, so he took a good look at the man before he ran off.

7. The wolf killed the heifer and the geese because they belonged to Grandpa.

8. Grandpa was very tired, so he let his grandson prepare supper.

9. When Grandpa told the boy to spring the traps and leave them, the boy realized he was sick.

10. The wolf looked surprised to see the boy because he expected to see the old man.

11. Since the boy thought that Grandpa would want to see the wolf, he dragged the animal to the house.

12. Grandpa did not believe that it was the same wolf because he didn't want to believe that the wolf was dead.

13. The boy worried that he had done something wrong when he saw the expression on Grandpa's face.

14. Grandpa decided to go back with the boy because he was feeling very weak.

15. After he saw how old and tired Grandpa was, the boy realized he was not really nine feet tall.

Word Mastery Exercise

Directions: Circle the letter of the word or phrase that best defines each of the words from "The Finish of Patsy Barnes" printed in *italics* below. Use the context of each word to help determine its meaning.

1. Mrs. Barnes was often called to school to explain why her son Patsy was a *truant*.

   (a) bad student   (b) troublemaker   (c) student who stays away from school

2. Education was *compulsory,* and Mrs. Barnes wanted Patsy to learn.

   (a) required by law   (b) at the student's choice   (c) very strict

3. The *burden* of making a living was not easy for Patsy's mother.

   (a) career   (b) impossible chance   (c) heavy weight

4. With all her hard work, she made only a *scanty* living.

   (a) very small   (b) daily   (c) comfortable

5. Patsy found it difficult to be *diplomatic* with the doctor, whom he didn't like.

   (a) generous with money   (b) careful and sensitive in one's dealings   (c) willing to pay attention

6. Patsy's *considerable* earnings from racing made it possible for him to get medicine for his mother.

   (a) rather small   (b) rather large   (c) regular

7. Patsy prayed that his mother would come safely through the *crisis* of her disease.

   (a) dangerous time   (b) operation   (c) medical treatment

8. In his *curious* racing suit of maroon and green silk, Patsy was a sight to see.

   (a) very bright   (b) not matched   (c) very strange

9. He was sorry he said anything, and a *stammering* Patsy had to tell the owner the story of his father and the horse.

   (a) talking unevenly   (b) very proud   (c) sad

10. Because he knew that the horse had good *endurance,* Patsy kept him running at top speed.

    (a) parents   (b) horses to race against   (c) ability to keep going

Bonus Activity: Here are some more homophones: **horse, hoarse.** On a separate piece of paper, write one sentence about Patsy Barnes, using each word.

Outlining

Before people write or speak, they must plan how they will organize their information. A good way to do that is to prepare an outline. An **outline** lists the main ideas. Under each main idea, it lists details that tell more about it.

Directions: Below are some details that belong in the outline below. Study the outline. Then decide which details belong under each topic. Put them in time order. Some details are already shown in the outline. Write in the others.

The Percheron, a very large French workhorse, came from the European Great Horse.

Roman soldiers were probably the first to bring horses into England in the first century B.C.

In America today, horses are used mostly for riding and racing.

Spanish explorers first brought horses to the New World in the sixteenth century.

The American standardbred is a riding horse that came from one English horse brought to the United States in 1788.

Many workhorses come from the European Great Horse, which was developed in the Middle Ages.

One of the last breeds of workhorses to be developed was the shire, an English horse.

The American saddle horse, a riding horse, was first recognized as a breed in the 1800s.

The Arabian horse is the ancestor of most breeds of riding horses.

Humans probably first began to use horses to pull war chariots about 4,000 years ago in the Near East.

On the Great Plains, American Indians found horses that had escaped from the Spanish explorers and learned to ride them.

The thoroughbred was developed in England as a riding and racing horse.

The Horse

I. History

   A. Horses in Europe and Asia

      1. _____

      2. _____

   B. Horses in the Americas

      1. _____

      2. _____

      3. _____

II. Workhorses

      1. _____

      2. _____

      3. _____

III. Riding Horses

    A. Near Eastern and European Breeds

        1. _____

        2. _____

    B. American Breeds

        1. _____

        2. _____

Word Mastery Exercise

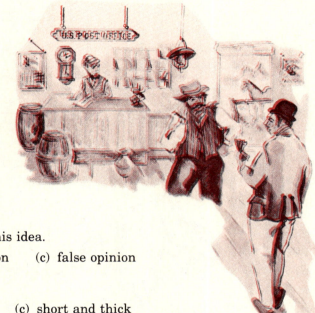

Directions: Circle the letter of the word or phrase that best defines each of the words from "The Substance and the Shadow" printed in *italics* below. Use the context of each word to help determine its meaning.

1. There was not very much *substance* to his idea.

    (a) important matter   (b) discussion   (c) false opinion

2. The stranger was a *stubby* little man.

    (a) acting odd   (b) very stubborn   (c) short and thick

3. The horse they rented was a bony *nag*.

    (a) mule   (b) constant complainer   (c) old, worn-out horse

4. The *compromise* they agreed on was that Jack would get half a horse and pay five dollars.

    (a) agreement in which each person gives up something
    (b) arrangement that is unfair to both people
    (c) arrangement that is unfair to everyone

5. Jack *observed* that the horse's shadow was a good place to be in the hot sun.

    (a) noticed   (b) did not think   (c) complained

Bonus Activity: The word *shadow* has many meanings. Read the five that are listed below. Then read the sentences. Write the letter of the meaning used on the blanks next to the sentences.

_____ 6. There was just a *shadow* of doubt about his honesty.	**a.** area of shade caused by something coming between a light and the area
_____ 7. They stood in the *shadow* of the tree to keep cool.	**b.** something that has no reality
_____ 8. The chief asked the detective to *shadow* the criminal.	**c.** a faint suggestion
_____ 9. The roof *shadows* her features and makes them hard to see.	**d.** to throw a shadow on
_____ 10. Their dream of riches was just a *shadow* that never came true.	**e.** to follow closely, trying not to be seen

Identifying Topic and Theme

(Keyed to "The Substance and the Shadow" Pages 320–323)

A. Directions: Which of the following could be a theme for a story? Which could be a topic? Write *topic* or *theme* on the blank next to each.

1. The Fourth of July   _____

2. Since the United States was born, fireworks have been used to celebrate the Fourth of July.   _____

3. Some people care more about the shadow than the substance.   _____

4. Reaching a compromise   _____

5. Age and youth   _____

6. People who cheat others often worry about being cheated themselves.   _____

7. Foolish arguments   _____

8. Keeping half is better than losing all.   _____

9. Understanding fables   _____

10. Fables are a good way of teaching a lesson.   _____

B. Directions: Choose a theme for each of the topics below. Write the theme as a complete sentence.

1. My Favorite Sport

_____

_____

2. Planning Ahead

_____

_____

Word Mastery Exercise

Directions: Circle the letter of the word or phrase that best defines each of the words from "The Man Who Was a Horse" printed in *italics* below. Use the context of each word to help determine its meaning.

1. Bob was especially good at catching *mustangs* on the plains.

   (a) wild horses   (b) wild cattle   (c) wild buffalo

2. After riding several hours, he *dismounted* and made his camp for the night.

   (a) pitched a tent   (b) got off his horse   (c) made a fire

3. He wanted to *dispute* the idea that stars were distant suns.

   (a) argue   (b) agree with   (c) think about

4. He told time by watching the *arc* of the sun's path.

   (a) burning heat   (b) sailing direction   (c) part of a circle

5. He filled his *canteen* at the river.

   (a) food bag   (b) water container   (c) cowboy hat

6. Without much *hesitation,* the stallion and the other horses accepted Bob as if he were a horse.

   (a) stopping before acting   (b) wild anger   (c) noises that horses make

7. At the *critical* moment, Bob took over the stallion's job as leader of the herd.

   (a) planned in advance   (b) very important   (c) unexpected

8. No other cowboys could *reproduce* Bob's success at catching mustangs.

   (a) explain   (b) object to   (c) copy

9. After they were tamed, the mustangs began to *mingle* with the other horses.

   (a) mix together   (b) fight   (c) try to escape

Bonus Activity: While reading "The Man Who Was a Horse," you learned several words from context. Choose one of the words listed below and write a sentence using it.

      intense   mesa   relinquish   taut

_____

_____

Distinguishing Between Fact and Opinion ___

(Keyed to "The Man Who Was a Horse" Pages 325–333)

> **Facts** are statements that you can check and prove to be true or false. For example, it is a fact that Bob Lemmons was a cowboy.
> **Opinions** are what people believe. Opinions cannot be proved. For example, it is an opinion that Bob Lemmons was the finest cowboy on his ranch.

Directions: Below are 20 statements about "The Man Who Was a Horse." For each statement circle **F** (fact) or **O** (opinion). You may look back at the selection if you like.

1. **F O** The land around the ranch was very flat.

2. **F O** Bob should have taught some of the other cowboys how to catch mustangs.

3. **F O** Bob Lemmons, a black cowboy, was a real person.

4. **F O** A suspicious stallion is a lot of trouble.

5. **F O** The only good way to bring in a herd of wild mustangs was to act like a horse.

6. **F O** Bob Lemmons was a slave until he was freed in 1865.

7. **F O** Wild mustangs are a beautiful sight.

8. **F O** Everybody knew that one man could not catch a herd of mustangs.

9. **F O** Pilar's father would not let her marry Bob.

10. **F O** Bob spent many days losing his human odor before he went near the mustangs.

11. **F O** Texas was probably the hottest place in the world.

12. **F O** The high mountains are the loveliest part of Wyoming.

13. **F O** The mustangs were smaller than Bob's own horse.

14. **F O** Mustangs are better horses than those born on ranches.

15. **F O** Bob spent two weeks leading the herd of mustangs.

16. **F O** Bob was gone from the ranch for almost a month before he brought the mustangs in.

17. **F O** No one can ever get to understand a mustang by riding it.

18. **F O** Bob told the cowboys to get the corral ready for the mustangs.

19. **F O** Bob's food was left for him in the west pasture.

20. **F O** Once captured, the mustangs were only horses.

Designing a Cattle Brand

(Keyed to "The Man Who Was a Horse" Pages 325–333)

> The word *brand*, which we now use to mean the name of a company or a product, comes from a word meaning "burning stick." Cattle ranches brand cattle by burning special symbols on them to show who owns the animals. Each ranch has its own symbol, called a *brand*. A good brand should be hard for someone else to change. For example, if a brand is a simple triangle, someone else could brand a circle inside or outside the triangle to change it. So a good brand should be somewhat complicated.

Directions: Design your own cattle brand by following the directions below.

1. First, choose a name for your ranch. It could have something to do with your own name. For example, if your last name is Fox, you might want to have "fox" in the ranch name. The name could have something to do with nature. You could use "two pines" or "three crows" or "lightning." Write the name of your ranch below.

_____

2. Think about something in your own name that you can use in the brand. Your initials might be good. What can you use from your initials or name?

_____

3. Now draw a simple design with thick lines. Start with one or more initials, something in the ranch name, or a shape such as a circle or a zigzag.

My Brand

4. Add something to your drawing to make it hard for someone to change it. Now give a name to your brand. Some examples would be "Twin Pines," "Double E," or "Circle R."

_____

Word Mastery Exercise

(Keyed to "Amelia's Bloomers" Page 345–350)

Directions: Circle the letter of the word or phrase that best defines each of the words from "Amelia's Bloomers" printed in *italics* below. Use the context of each word to help determine its meaning.

1. Many people made fun of the *bloomers* that some of the women were wearing.

    (a) flowered hats   (b) loose pants   (c) jogging suits

2. The long dresses with tight waists were too *cumbersome* to allow women to move easily.

    (a) difficult to manage   (b) loose and ugly   (c) of poor quality

3. Elizabeth continued to wear her Turkish outfit in spite of the *glares* of her neighbors.

    (a) nasty remarks   (b) angry looks   (c) complaints to police

4. The teenage boys on the streets *taunted* the women whenever they wore their new clothes.

    (a) threw stones at   (b) whistled at   (c) made fun of

5. Elizabeth explained to her son that the clothing most women wore was *inconvenient* and dangerous.

    (a) against the law   (b) easy to tear   (c) troublesome

Bonus Activity: The prefix *in-* usually means "not." The spelling of the prefix *in-* is changed to *il-* before an *l, ir-* before an *r,* or *im-* before an *m, p,* or *b.* Often, adding the prefix *in-* changes a word into its antonym.

   Change each of the following words into its antonym by adding the correct form of the prefix *in-*. Then tell the meaning of the new word.

6. convenient: the word _____ means

   _____

7. possible: the word _____ means

   _____

8. responsible: the word _____ means

   _____

9. legal: the word _____ means

   _____

10. movable: the word _____ means

    _____

Words from People's Names

(Keyed to "Amelia's Bloomers" Pages 345–350)

Many articles of clothing are named after people. Often they are named after famous people who wore the clothing, not those who invented them. Bloomers, the loose pants women wore instead of skirts, were named after Amelia Bloomer. Cardigans are sweaters that button or zip up the front and usually do not have a collar. They are named for James Thomas Brudenell (1797–1868), the 7th Earl of Cardigan, an English general. Raglan sleeves start under the arm and continue in a slanted line to the neck. Usually a raglan sleeve is looser than other sleeves. Raglan sleeves are named for F. J. H. Somerset (1788–1855), Lord Raglan, a British military commander. Wellington boots are high boots that are usually higher (above the knee) in front and lower in the back. They take their name from Arthur Wellesley (1769–1852), 1st Duke of Wellington, a British general and prime minister.

Directions: Remember that when you skim, you read quickly to find the information you need. Read the questions following the paragraph, then skim through the paragraph to find answers.

1. What was the title of the man for whom cardigans were named? _____

2. What was the personal name of the man for whom cardigans were named? _____

3. What was F. J. H. Somerset's title? _____

4. What style of clothing was named for F. J. H Somerset? _____

5. For whom were Wellington boots named? (Give the name and the title.) _____

6. What two occupations did Wellesley have? _____ and _____

7. When did Wellesley live? _____

8. Was Lord Raglan born before or after the Duke of Wellington? _____

Word Mastery Exercise

Directions: Circle the letter of the word or phrase that best defines each of the words from "The Parable of the Eagle" printed in *italics* below. Use the context of each word to help determine its meaning.

1. The story of the eagle who was treated like a chicken is a *parable*.

    (a) story that teaches a lesson   (b) story that cannot be true   (c) difficult idea to understand

2. The *naturalist* enjoyed taking groups of students to look at the woods.

    (a) person who eats wild plants   (b) person who never went to school   (c) person who studies plants and animals

3. "Eagle," he said, "*behold* the sun!"

    (a) look at   (b) fly up to   (c) try to catch

4. Before long, the eagle's body began to *tremble*.

    (a) grow cold   (b) shake   (c) flap its wings

5. The eagle soon *soared* into the sky.

    (a) sang   (b) stared   (c) flew high

Bonus Activity: One meaning for the suffix *-ist* is a person who does a particular kind of work or is good at a certain thing. Write the word on the blank that fits the definition given. (You may have to drop or change a letter.)

6. person who knows the natural world: _____

7. person who plays a violin: _____

8. person who is good at art: _____

9. person who writes novels: _____

10. person who studies science: _____

Identifying the Moral

(Keyed to "The Parable of the Eagle" Pages 353–354)

> Fables and parables are stories that usually have morals, which are intended to teach lessons. The moral should make sense if you know the story. Sometimes the moral is told with humor.

Directions: Match the moral to the fables. Write the letter of the moral next to the number of the fable.

_____ 1. An ant was thirsty and went to drink some water at a pond. He slipped, fell in, and nearly drowned. A dove was sitting nearby on a tree. She saw that the ant was in danger and dropped a leaf into the pond so the ant could use it for a raft. The ant climbed quickly onto the leaf and was saved.

Just then, the ant noticed a hunter going after the dove with a net. The hunter was barefoot, so the ant bit him on the heel. The hunter jumped, dropped his net, and the dove was able to fly to safety.

a. In unity there is strength.

b. Think twice before you leap.

_____ 2. A father had four sons who were always fighting. He tried to get them to stop, but nothing he said could convince them to change their ways. Then one day, he called them together. He showed them a bundle of sticks that he had tied together.

"Which of you can break this bundle of sticks in half?" he asked. Each son tried but could not break the bundle of sticks.

Then the father untied the bundle. He gave them each a single stick. "Can you break those?" he asked. Of course, they found they could break them easily.

"My sons," the father said, "you can learn from this bundle of sticks. If you remain united, you will be too strong for any enemy. But if you quarrel and are each alone, it will be easy for an enemy to destroy you."

c. Trouble comes from the direction we least expect.

d. One good turn deserves another.

e. If you are too greedy, you may end up with nothing.

_____ 3. A deer was blind in one eye and could not see from that side. So she was careful to spend most of her time on a cliff near the sea. That way, she could stand with her good eye, watching the land for hunters. Her blind eye faced the sea because she did not expect danger to come from the water.

One day, some hunters came by in a boat. They noticed the deer on the cliff. One of them shot her. As she was dying, the deer thought, "Poor me! I was safe from the land where I expected to find danger. Instead, my enemy came from the sea, where I expected to find protection."

_____ 4. A farmer had a goose that he kept for the eggs she laid. One day when he went to her nest, he found a solid gold egg. Very excited at his discovery, he ran and showed the egg to his wife.

The next day, he found another golden egg in the goose's nest. And for several more days, she laid eggs of pure gold.

But the farmer grew greedy. "If I cut open the goose," he thought, "I can get all her golden eggs at once."

So he cut the goose open and found no eggs inside. Worse, his wonderful goose was now dead.

_____ 5. It had been a dry summer without any rain. Two frogs went hopping down a road looking for water. At last they came to a deep well. One of the frogs grew very excited. He was about to dive into the well.

"Wait!" said the other. "This well is very deep. What if it is dry like everything else? Then we'll have no water and no way of getting out."

The two frogs decided to continue looking for water.

Word Mastery Exercise

Directions: Circle the letter of the word or phrase that best defines each of the words from "The Pathway from Slavery to Freedom" printed in *italics* below. Use the context of each word to help determine its meaning.

1. Douglass understood that slavery *dehumanizes* people.

   (a) makes kind   (b) treats cruelly   (c) is bad for

2. He couldn't understand how a *pious* person could own slaves.

   (a) religious   (b) poor   (c) free

3. Mr. Auld thought that it was *irresponsible* to teach a slave to read.

   (a) not kind   (b) not a bad idea   (c) not responsible

4. Douglass considered slavery an *infernal* situation.

   (a) inside the soul   (b) of the devil   (c) based on error

5. Frederick's reading lessons had led to *discord* between Mr. and Mrs. Auld.

   (a) a better understanding   (b) pleasant conversation   (c) a lack of harmony

6. Frederick realized that it was *injurious* to him to keep him from learning to read.

   (a) preventing injury   (b) harmful   (c) unwise

7. The *opposition* of Mr. Auld strengthened Frederick's desire to read.

   (a) chance given   (b) encouragement   (c) strong position against

8. Mrs. Auld was forced to *acknowledge* that she had been wrong.

   (a) admit   (b) deny   (c) guess

9. Education and slavery are *incompatible*.

   (a) impossible to imagine   (b) against the law
   (c) not in agreement with each other

10. Frederick *resolved* that he would read, and he went about learning how to do it.

    (a) decided   (b) wished   (c) hoped

Bonus Activity: Write a sentence about Frederick Douglass. In your sentence, use two of the words in *italics* above.

_____

_____

Recognizing Settings

(Keyed to "The Pathway from Slavery to Freedom" Pages 357–361)

Directions: Setting often create a mood. Decide what kind of mood each setting below tries to create. Then write the word from the word box that best describes that mood.

adventurous	boring	cheerful
nervous	scary	unpleasant

1. An owl hooted through the dark branches. Strange things brushed against my face. A smell I couldn't identify brought to my mind a memory of years ago. And the clock far off in the bell tower showed midnight. _____

2. The spaceship was new and shiny. Maps of different parts of the universe showed on the TV screens. Exciting music played as the young space cadets marched on board. There was a feeling in the air that something new and important was about to happen. _____

3. The streets were gray and damp. The sky was gray and cloudy. Most of the people who walked along the streets were wearing gray. Even the buildings and trees seemed to be of the same dull gray material that made up the natural environment. _____

4. Bright sun streamed through the window and fell on a singing canary hopping about his cage. The flowers on the table seemed to welcome anyone who walked in. Smells of apple pie and roasting turkey drifted through the air. _____

5. The room looked as if a tornado had just swept through it. Piles of papers, dirty cups that had once been filled with coffee, and dirty socks were everywhere. We all held handkerchiefs over our noses to keep out the smell. _____

6. Tick, tick, tick. The clock seemed very loud in the quiet room. At each desk sat one student with pencils, erasers, and test papers. All one could hear besides the sound of the clock were the sharp heels of the monitor walking around the room. _____

Proofreading

(Keyed to "The Pathway from Slavery to Freedom" Pages 357–361)

Work written for others to read should always be checked for mistakes in spelling, usage, and punctuation. Reading to correct errors is called **proofreading.** When an error is found, it should be crossed out and the correction made just above it.

Directions: Here is a selection about Frederick Douglass for you to proofread. Correct all **sentence fragments** (incomplete sentences) and **run-on sentences** (two sentences incorrectly written as one). Look for incorrect spellings, missing or incorrect punctuation, and incorrect words. Add any missing words. Write the revised paragraph on the lines below.

Fredericks mistress soon began to follow her husband's advise. She became worse than her husband she was not happy jist to follow his orders. She wanted to be even worser. The site of Frederick with a newspaper threw her into a furry. he still keeped trying to learn read. Young friends he met in the streets helped learn him. Frederick got his lessons were he could. He all ways took a book. and some bread to give to the other boys. who were very hungry. He was hungry for read. He also planed to learn to right.

_____

_____

_____

_____

_____

_____

_____

_____

Word Mastery Exercise

Directions: Circle the letter of the word or phrase that best defines each of the words from "The Big Wave" printed in *italics* below. Use the context of each word to help determine its meaning.

1. Kino's mother usually wore a *kimono*.

    (a) loose slacks (b) fancy hat (c) Japanese robe

2. It was time to begin to *reap* the wheat.

    (a) gather (b) plant (c) water

3. The *incessant* ringing of the bell warned the people of danger.

    (a) loud (b) out of tune (c) without stopping

4. He bowed as he crossed the *threshold* of the cottage.

    (a) living room (b) entrance (c) garden

5. The old gentleman kept some poems in an *alcove* in his house.

    (a) window (b) locked box (c) small room

Bonus Activity: You can make many words by combining *sea* with another word. Figure out the word that begins with *sea* and fits the definition. The blanks tell you how many letters are in each answer.

6. fish or shellfish that people eat: __ __ __ __ __ __ __

7. city that ships from the sea use as a harbor: __ __ __ __ __ __ __ __

8. hard part of a sea animal, such as a clam or conch: __ __ __ __ __ __ __ __ __

9. suffering from the motion of the sea: __ __ __ __ __ __ __

10. beach area near the sea: __ __ __ __ __ __ __ __

Recognizing Literary Genres

(Keyed to "The Big Wave" Pages 366–388)

The word **genre** means "type" or "kind." When we talk about literary genres, we may organize the types into groups such as short stories, fiction, nonfiction, plays, and poems. From here, we may further organize them into mysteries, comedies, legends, myths, and fables.

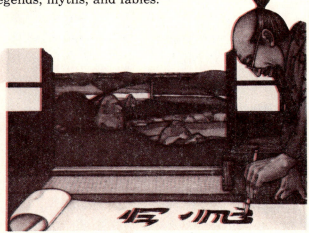

A. Directions: Pick the word from the word box that best describes the genre of each sample on this page.

autobiography	biography	short story	play	poem

_____ 1. The glories of our blood and state
Are shadows, not substantial things.
There is nor armor against fate;
Death lays his icy hands on kings.

_____ 2.   I was born in Boston in 1823. My father was a sea captain, and my mother was the daughter of a man who owned many sailing ships.

_____ 3.   Scene 2
Marian: (*falling*) Ow! I hurt my ankle.
Owen: (*offering to help her up*) Does it pain you much?
Marian: Only when I put my weight on it. I think I'll
be able to walk in a minute or two.

_____ 4.   "This is going to be harder than I expected," Sam thought.
He rang the bell, and Carrie's mother came to the door.
   "Carrie has been in an accident," he said "She's at the hospital now."

_____ 5.   At the age of 17, Benjamin Franklin left his home in Boston and went to Philadelphia. There he worked for several different printers. In 1729, he bought a printing business and started to publish his own paper.

B. Directions: Pick the word from the word box that best describes the genre of each sample on this page.

fable	legend	mystery	myth	science fiction

_____ **6.** Just a few minutes before, everybody had stood around admiring the prize-winning painting. Now it was gone. Nobody had come into the room, and nobody had left. What had happened to the painting?

_____ **7.** Qix sealed his spacesuit and opened the door of the spaceship. It looked like it was going to be another dull day on Saturn.
  Suddenly, he heard a whirring sound. The thing coming toward him did not look like any spaceship he had seen before. It headed straight toward him, then turned just before it would have struck his chest.

_____ **8.** Arachne wove beautiful clothes. She began to think that she was the greatest weaver in the world.
  "I am a greater weaver," she said, "than the goddess Athena."
  Athena heard Arachne and grew very angry. Swiftly she changed Arachne into a spider.
  "Now you can weave all day long," she told Arachne.

_____ **9.** Stormalong was a sailor in the days of ships with sails. He was about 14 fathoms tall and he could handle almost anything. When a huge octopus threatened his ship, Stormalong wrestled it and tied its arms into knots. He ate his soup from a boat, and he had four ostrich eggs for breakfast every day.

_____ **10.** The cat grabbed for the bird and caught it. "If you let me go," said the bird, "I'll tell you where you can get two birds on a bush nearby." The greedy cat decided that two birds were better than one. So he let the first bird go. As she flew out of the cat's reach, the bird called out, "If you look in the bushes, you may find some other birds." That night the cat went without dinner.
  Moral: A bird in the hand is worth two in the bush.

Paraphrasing to Change Play Forms to Narrative

(Keyed to "The Big Wave" Pages 366–388)

Directions: "The Big Wave" was first written as a story. Then the author turned it into a play for radio. Your job is to turn a section of the play back into part of a short story. In other words, change the play form into story form.

Rewrite Act Three (pages 375–376) as part of a story. You do not have to include everything, just the main idea. Write it in your own way, using your own words. When you are finished, proofread it to correct any mistakes.

_____

_____

_____

_____

_____

_____

_____

_____

_____

_____

_____

_____

_____

_____

_____

_____

_____

_____

_____

_____

_____

_____

Reviewing Important Ideas

Directions: Match the terms in the column on the left with the definitions in the column on the right. Write the letter of the definition on the blank next to the term.

_____ 1. antonyms

_____ 2. author's purpose

_____ 3. cause

_____ 4. choral reading

_____ 5. climax

_____ 6. conflict

_____ 7. dialogue

_____ 8. effect

_____ 9. exaggeration

_____ 10. five W's

_____ 11. idiom

_____ 12. narrative

_____ 13. oral interpretation

_____ 14. paraphrase

_____ 15. rising action

_____ 16. supporting details

_____ 17. synonyms

_____ 18. time order

_____ 19. turning point

_____ 20. visualizing

a. words said by characters
b. words that tell a story
c. statement that makes something seem bigger or more important
d. event or idea that leads to a result
e. result that is brought about by an event or idea
f. reason an author has for writing
g. reading aloud in a group
h. words that mean the same
i. words that mean the opposite
j. problem that a character must overcome
k. forming a picture in your mind
l. the turning point in a story, the most exciting part
m. the high point of action
n. an expression that means something different from what the words seem to say
o. the order in which events take place
p. who, what, when, where, why
q. reading aloud with expression
r. increasing tension in a story
s. say something in your own words
t. statements that support the main idea

Reviewing Literary Terms

A. Directions: Here is a list of terms you used in discussing the selections in the book. Match each term to its definition. Then write the term in the puzzle. When you are done, the word in the column under the arrow will be something you have studied this year.

character	comparison	conclusion	contrast	foreshadowing
inference	plot	setting	theme	topic

1. The action that happens in a story
2. What a story is about
3. When and where a story takes place
4. The basic idea of a piece of writing
5. Person or creature in a story
6. Showing how things are alike
7. Showing how things are different
8. Ending of a story
9. Figuring out something not stated in a story
10. Hinting at something that will happen later

B. Directions: Answer the following questions in your own words.

Who was your favorite character in the selections you read?

_____

Why was that your favorite character?

_____

What was your favorite story in this anthology?

_____

What did you particularly like about the story?

_____